The Giant Book of Strange Facts

by
Jake Jacobs

* * * * *

Published by Jake Jacobs

1.

The Los Alamos Ranch House is located in Los Alamos, New Mexico, and served as the residence of the director of the Los Alamos Laboratory during the Manhattan Project.

2.

The house was originally built in 1917 as a guest ranch and later purchased by the University of California for use by the Manhattan Project.

3.

The Los Alamos Ranch House was designated as a National Historic Landmark in 1965.

4.

The house was known as "Bathtub Row" due to its location on the row of houses that had bathtubs, a luxury during that time.

5.

The Los Alamos Ranch House provided accommodation for some of the leading scientists and researchers involved in the development of the atomic bomb.

6.

The house played a central role in the Manhattan Project, as it was where many of the key decisions regarding the project were made.

7.

The Los Alamos Ranch House was the residence of J. Robert Oppenheimer, the scientific director of the Los Alamos Laboratory and one of the key figures of the Manhattan Project.

8.

The house served as a meeting place for scientists, engineers, and military officials involved in the project, fostering collaboration and exchange of ideas.

9.

The Los Alamos Ranch House is a classic Pueblo Revival style building, reflecting the architectural style prevalent in the region.

10.

The house features adobe walls, vigas (wooden beams), and kiva fireplaces, which are characteristic of traditional Pueblo architecture.

11.

The Los Alamos Ranch House has a tranquil and scenic location, surrounded by the beautiful landscape of the Jemez Mountains.

12.

The house has a significant historical and cultural value as it represents the critical period of the Manhattan Project and the scientific advancements achieved during that time.

13.

Today, the Los Alamos Ranch House is part of the Los Alamos Historical Museum and is open to the public as a historic site.

14.

The house contains exhibits and displays that provide insights into the history of the Manhattan Project and the role of Los Alamos in the development of atomic weapons.

15.

The Los Alamos Ranch House has been carefully preserved to maintain its original architectural integrity and historical significance.

16.

Visitors to the house can explore the rooms where key discussions and decisions regarding the atomic bomb took place.

17.

The Los Alamos Ranch House offers a glimpse into the daily lives of the scientists and their families who lived and worked in Los Alamos during the project.

18.

The house has been the subject of various books and documentaries, highlighting its significance in the context of the Manhattan Project.

19.

The Los Alamos Ranch House serves as a reminder of the ethical and moral dilemmas associated with the development and use of atomic weapons.

20.

The house's location in Los Alamos, a secluded area, was chosen for its remoteness and security during the Manhattan Project.

21.

The Los Alamos Ranch House played a pivotal role in the successful completion of the atomic bomb, which had a profound impact on world history.

22.

The Los Alamos Ranch House showcases the living conditions and lifestyle of the scientists and their families during the intense period of scientific research and development.

23.

The house's architecture reflects a blend of traditional Pueblo design and the influence of Spanish colonial style prevalent in the region.

24.

The Los Alamos Ranch House offers visitors a chance to gain a deeper understanding of the challenges and sacrifices made by the scientists involved in the Manhattan Project.

25.

The Los Alamos Ranch House is surrounded by a picturesque landscape, making it an attractive destination for history and nature enthusiasts alike.

26.

The house is often visited by scholars, researchers, and students interested in the history of the Manhattan Project and the development of atomic weapons.

27.

The Los Alamos Ranch House is a symbol of scientific ingenuity, showcasing the collaborative efforts of brilliant minds working towards a common goal.

28.

The house has witnessed historic moments, such as the successful Trinity nuclear test, which took place in July 1945, marking the first detonation of an atomic bomb.

29.

The Los Alamos Ranch House has a visitor center where guests can learn more about the history of the house, the Manhattan Project, and the impact of atomic weapons.

30.

The Los Alamos Ranch House has been featured in various films, documentaries, and television shows that explore the history and legacy of the Manhattan Project.

31.

The house serves as a memorial to the scientists and researchers who worked in Los Alamos and their contributions to science and technology.

32.

The Los Alamos Ranch House has been recognized as an important cultural and historical site, preserving the memory of the groundbreaking scientific advancements made during World War II.

33.

The house's strategic location in Los Alamos provided a secure and controlled environment for the highly sensitive research and development activities of the Manhattan Project.

34.

The Los Alamos Ranch House has a small garden area where visitors can relax and enjoy the peaceful surroundings.

35.

The house's interior is furnished with period-appropriate furniture and artifacts, allowing visitors to step back in time and experience the atmosphere of the Manhattan Project era.

36.

The Los Alamos Ranch House hosts educational programs and events to engage visitors of all ages in learning about the history of the house and the scientific breakthroughs that took place there.

37.

The house has become a symbol of the ethical and moral questions surrounding the use of nuclear weapons and the responsibility of scientists in the pursuit of knowledge.

38.

The Los Alamos Ranch House attracts visitors from around the world who are interested in understanding the scientific, historical, and ethical aspects of the Manhattan Project.

39.

The Los Alamos Ranch House is an integral part of the larger Los Alamos National Laboratory complex, which continues to conduct important scientific research and development today.

40.

The house provides a window into the personal lives and experiences of the scientists, revealing their dedication, challenges, and sacrifices during the Manhattan Project.

41.

The Los Alamos Ranch House stands as a testament to human curiosity and the pursuit of scientific knowledge, while also raising important questions about the responsible use of that knowledge.

42.

The house offers guided tours, led by knowledgeable docents, who provide detailed insights into the history and significance of the Manhattan Project and the Los Alamos community.

43.

The Los Alamos Ranch House has been recognized for its architectural significance, representing a blend of indigenous and colonial influences.

44.

The house's location in the scenic mountains of New Mexico provides visitors with a serene and peaceful environment to reflect upon the history and implications of the Manhattan Project.

45.

The Los Alamos Ranch House stands as a reminder of the immense power of scientific discovery and the responsibility to use that power wisely and ethically.

46.

The house's museum exhibits showcase artifacts, photographs, and documents related to the Manhattan Project, giving visitors a comprehensive understanding of the project's scope and impact.

47.

The Los Alamos Ranch House has become an important destination for history buffs, scientists, and those interested in the intersection of science, technology, and society.

48.

The house's architecture and design reflect the region's cultural heritage, paying homage to the Native American and Spanish influences that shaped the area's history.

49.

The Los Alamos Ranch House offers visitors a unique opportunity to delve into the complex history of nuclear weapons and their role in shaping the modern world.

50.

The house's legacy extends beyond its physical structure, representing the collective efforts of countless individuals who worked diligently and often under intense pressure to develop groundbreaking scientific advancements.

51.

The Los Angeles Memorial Coliseum, often referred to as "The Coliseum," is located in Exposition Park in Los Angeles, California.

52.

The Coliseum is a historic sports stadium and has been the site of numerous significant events, including the Olympic Games and Super Bowls.

53.

It was originally constructed in 1923 as a memorial to the veterans of World War I.

54.

The Coliseum has a seating capacity of over 77,000, making it one of the largest stadiums in the United States.

55.

It is the home stadium for the University of Southern California (USC) Trojans football team.

56.

The Coliseum has hosted the Summer Olympic Games twice: in 1932 and 1984.

57.

It is the only stadium to have hosted the Summer Olympic Games twice.

58.

During the 1932 Olympics, the Coliseum became the first stadium in history to have an Olympic Village for athletes.

59.

The Coliseum played a significant role in the civil rights movement when it became the first integrated stadium in the United States.

60.

In 1963, Martin Luther King Jr. delivered his famous "I Have a Dream" speech at the Coliseum during a Civil Rights Movement rally.

61.

The Coliseum has also been the site of numerous concerts, political rallies, and cultural events.

62.

It has hosted several memorable musical performances, including concerts by The Rolling Stones, The Beatles, and Pink Floyd.

63.

The Coliseum was designated a National Historic Landmark in 1984.

64.

In addition to football and Olympic events, the Coliseum has hosted professional baseball, soccer, and track and field events.

65.

The Los Angeles Raiders, a former NFL team, called the Coliseum their home from 1982 to 1994.

66.

The Coliseum hosted the first Super Bowl in 1967, where the Green Bay Packers defeated the Kansas City Chiefs.

67.

It was the site of the 1959 World Series, where the Los Angeles Dodgers defeated the Chicago White Sox.

68.

The Coliseum has undergone several renovations and expansions over the years to enhance its facilities and accommodate larger crowds.

69.

It has a distinctive peristyle arch and torch tower entrance, which serves as an iconic symbol of the stadium.

70.

The Coliseum's field has a unique layout, as it is oriented diagonally, rather than parallel to the seating sections.

71.

The Coliseum has a rich sports history and has seen many legendary athletes compete on its grounds, including Jackie Robinson, O.J. Simpson, and Reggie Bush.

72.

It has been used as a filming location for numerous movies and television shows, including "Rocky III" and "The Naked Gun."

73.

The Coliseum has a rich tradition of hosting the annual Los Angeles County Holiday Celebration, a free concert featuring performances by various local artists and groups.

74.

It has been the venue for several political events and speeches by prominent figures, including presidents and political candidates.

75.

The Coliseum was the first stadium to host the World Series, the Super Bowl, and the Summer Olympics.

76.

The torch at the top of the peristyle arch is lit during USC Trojans home football games and other special events.

77.

The Coliseum played a significant role in the development of American football, as it hosted the first-ever NFL playoff game in 1933.

78.

The stadium has witnessed historic moments in sports, including record-breaking performances and championship victories.

79.

The Coliseum has been recognized for its architectural significance, blending elements of classical and modern design.

80.

It has been praised for its ability to accommodate large crowds while providing excellent sightlines and acoustics for sporting events and concerts.

81.

The Coliseum served as a temporary home for the Los Angeles Rams during their return to the city in 2016 before moving to their own stadium.

82.

The Coliseum has a rich cultural legacy and is considered a symbol of Los Angeles and its vibrant sports and entertainment scene.

83.

The Coliseum has hosted several major international soccer matches, including the FIFA World Cup and the CONCACAF Gold Cup.

84.

It has been the site of memorable moments in soccer history, including Pelé's final competitive match in 1977.

85.

The Coliseum's close proximity to downtown Los Angeles and other cultural attractions makes it a popular destination for tourists and locals alike.

86.

The stadium has been praised for its sustainable initiatives, including the use of solar panels and recycling programs.

87.

The Coliseum has a unique blend of history and modern amenities, offering visitors a glimpse into the past while providing a comfortable and enjoyable experience.

88.

It has been a venue for major music festivals, such as the Electric Daisy Carnival and the Hard Summer Music Festival.

89.

The Coliseum has a rich tradition of tailgating before football games, creating a vibrant and festive atmosphere.

90.

The stadium's iconic arches and columns make it a visually striking landmark in the Los Angeles skyline.

91.

The Coliseum has hosted multiple editions of the X Games, showcasing extreme sports and attracting athletes and fans from around the world.

92.

The stadium has been the site of various charity events and fundraisers, leveraging its popularity to support worthy causes.

93.

The Coliseum has been featured in popular culture, including appearances in movies, music videos, and television shows.

94.

The stadium has hosted major religious events, such as Billy Graham crusades and religious conventions.

95.

The Coliseum's location within Exposition Park allows visitors to explore other nearby attractions, such as the Natural History Museum of Los Angeles County and the California Science Center.

96.

The Coliseum has a rich tradition of hosting college football rivalries, including the USC vs. UCLA game, known as the "Battle for the Victory Bell."

97.

The stadium's design incorporates elements inspired by ancient Greek and Roman architecture, adding a sense of grandeur and elegance.

98.

The Coliseum has hosted multiple international track and field competitions, including the World Athletics Championships.

99.

The stadium's historical significance and architectural beauty make it a popular venue for weddings and special events.

100.

The Coliseum has become an iconic symbol of sports and entertainment in Los Angeles, representing the city's passion for athletics, history, and cultural diversity.

101.

Deer belong to the family Cervidae, which includes over 90 species worldwide.

102.

They are found on every continent except Antarctica.

103.

The white-tailed deer is the most widespread deer species in North America.

104.

Male deer, called bucks, grow and shed their antlers annually.

105.

Antlers are one of the fastest-growing tissues in the animal kingdom, growing up to an inch per day.

106.

Female deer, called does, do not have antlers.

107.

Deer have excellent hearing and can rotate their ears independently to detect sounds from different directions.

108.

They also have a keen sense of smell, which helps them detect predators and find food.

109.

Deer have specialized stomachs that allow them to digest a wide variety of plant material.

110.

They are herbivores and primarily feed on leaves, grasses, fruits, and nuts.

111.

Deer are excellent jumpers and can leap over obstacles up to 10 feet high.

112.

They are also strong swimmers and can cover long distances in the water.

113.

Deer have a unique behavior called rutting, which is the mating season characterized by males competing for mates.

114.

During the rut, bucks engage in aggressive behaviors such as antler wrestling and vocalizations to establish dominance.

115.

Deer have a specialized gland on their hind legs called the metatarsal gland, which releases a scent used for communication.

116.

Fawns, or baby deer, are born with white spots on their fur, which help camouflage them in their surroundings.

117.

Does typically give birth to one or two fawns at a time.

118.

Fawns can stand and walk within a few hours of being born.

119.

Deer have a keen sense of danger and can quickly flee from predators by reaching speeds of up to 40 miles per hour.

120.

They have a natural instinct to freeze when they sense danger, relying on their excellent camouflage to avoid detection.

121.

Deer have a four-chambered stomach, similar to cows, which allows them to efficiently extract nutrients from their plant-based diet.

122.

Deer are known to migrate over long distances in search of food and favorable breeding conditions.

123.

They have a lifespan of around 10 to 15 years in the wild.

124.

Deer have large eyes positioned on the sides of their head, providing them with a wide field of vision to detect potential threats.

125.

They have specialized muscles in their eyes that enable them to see well in low light conditions.

126.

Deer communicate through various vocalizations, including grunts, bleats, and snorts.

127.

They also communicate non-verbally through body language, such as tail flicking and ear movements.

128.

Deer have a unique ability to rotate their eyes independently, allowing them to scan their surroundings for predators.

129.

They shed their fur twice a year, transitioning from a thicker winter coat to a lighter summer coat.

130.

Deer are known for their ability to adapt to different habitats, ranging from forests and grasslands to mountains and deserts.

131.

They are important to ecosystems as they help disperse seeds through their droppings and browsing habits.

132.

Deer are susceptible to a variety of diseases, including chronic wasting disease and tick-borne illnesses.

133.

They have a strong sense of social hierarchy within their herds, with dominant individuals having access to the best resources.

134.

Deer have a specialized chewing motion called rumination, where they regurgitate and re-chew their food for better digestion.

135.

They have a scent gland on their hind feet called the tarsal gland, which they use to leave scent markings on vegetation and other objects.

136.

Deer have a strong maternal instinct, with does fiercely protecting their fawns from predators.

137.

They are known for their agility and nimbleness, allowing them to navigate through dense vegetation and rough terrains.

138.

Deer have been depicted in various mythologies and folklore around the world, often symbolizing grace, fertility, and gentleness.

139.

In some cultures, deer are considered sacred animals and are associated with spiritual and mystical qualities.

140.

Deer populations are managed through hunting regulations to maintain a balance with their habitat and prevent overpopulation.

141.

Deer have adapted to human presence and can be found in suburban areas and even urban parks.

142.

They are known to cause damage to crops and gardens when their population density is high.

143.

Deer have a strong bond with their offspring, with does nursing and caring for their fawns until they are independent.

144.

They have a specialized adaptation called the Jacobson's organ, located in the roof of their mouth, which enhances their sense of smell.

145.

Deer are sensitive to ultrasonic sounds and can detect high-frequency noises beyond the range of human hearing.

146.

Deer are often the subject of wildlife conservation efforts, as their populations have been affected by habitat loss and fragmentation.

147.

They have been introduced to various regions around the world for hunting and ornamental purposes.

148.

Deer have been featured in literature, art, and folklore, symbolizing different qualities such as gentleness, beauty, and freedom.

149.

Various species of deer have unique physical characteristics, such as the large antlers of the moose and the impressive neck mane of the sika deer.

150.

Deer are fascinating creatures that have captivated humans for centuries, inspiring curiosity and admiration for their grace, resilience, and beauty.

151.

Degus are small rodents native to Chile and are closely related to guinea pigs and chinchillas.

152.

They have a stocky body with a short tail and can grow to be around 6 to 10 inches long.

153.

Degus are highly social animals and live in large family groups called colonies.

154.

They are diurnal, which means they are most active during the day.

155.

Degus have a unique vocalization system and can make a variety of sounds to communicate with each other.

156.

They are known for their agility and can jump and climb with ease.

157.

Degus have long, curved incisors that continuously grow throughout their lives.

158.
They use their teeth for gnawing on wood and other materials to keep them trimmed.

159.
Degus have a lifespan of around 6 to 8 years in captivity, but can live longer with proper care.

160.
In the wild, they primarily inhabit dry, rocky areas and are adapted to survive in harsh desert-like environments.

161.
Degus have a distinctive sandy brown fur with a lighter underbelly.

162.
They have a prehensile tail that they use for balance and climbing.

163.
Degus are herbivores and feed on a diet consisting mainly of grasses, seeds, and vegetation.

164.
They have specialized teeth and digestive systems that allow them to efficiently process their fibrous diet.

165.
Degus are known for their caching behavior, where they collect and store food in small burrows or crevices for later consumption.

166.
They have scent glands on their stomachs that they use to mark their territories.

167.

Degus are excellent diggers and construct complex burrow systems in their natural habitats.

168.

They are known for their curious and inquisitive nature, often exploring their surroundings and investigating new objects.

169.

Degus are monogamous animals and form long-term pair bonds with their mates.

170.

They communicate through a variety of vocalizations, including chirps, barks, and squeaks.

171.

Degus have a strong sense of smell and use scent marking to communicate with other members of their colony.

172.

They have a well-developed sense of hearing and can detect high-frequency sounds.

173.

Degus are known for their playful behavior, often engaging in chase games and wrestling with their colony mates.

174.

They are highly intelligent animals and can be trained to perform simple tricks and tasks.

175.

Degus are popular pets due to their social nature and their ability to form strong bonds with their owners.

176.

They require a spacious and enriched enclosure with plenty of hiding spots, climbing structures, and toys.

177.

Degus are sensitive to high temperatures and should be kept in a cool and well-ventilated environment.

178.

They are prone to dental problems, so it's important to provide them with a diet rich in hay and chew toys to promote dental health.

179.

Degus are capable of vocal mimicry and can imitate sounds from their environment.

180.

They are highly sensitive to changes in their environment and can become stressed easily.

181.

Degus have a unique behavior called "fur-slip," where they can shed patches of their fur as a defense mechanism when grabbed by predators.

182.

They have a keen sense of balance and can walk on narrow ledges and branches without falling.

183.

Degus have a well-developed grooming behavior and spend a significant amount of time cleaning their fur.

184.

They have a complex social hierarchy within their colonies, with dominant individuals having priority access to resources.

185.

Degus have been extensively studied in scientific research due to their social behavior and adaptability to captivity.

186.

They are known to exhibit communal parenting, where multiple adults in the colony help care for the young.

187.

Degus have a unique adaptation called "sunbathing," where they lie on their backs and expose their bellies to the sun to regulate their body temperature.

188.

They have a keen sense of spatial memory and can remember the location of food caches and familiar landmarks.

189.

Degus are susceptible to obesity and should be provided with a balanced diet and regular exercise.

190.

They are vulnerable to a variety of health conditions, including diabetes, dental issues, and respiratory infections.

191.

Degus have a relatively long gestation period of around 90 to 100 days.

192.

They give birth to litters of 1 to 10 pups, with an average litter size of 4 to 6.

193.

Degu pups are born fully furred with their eyes open and are able to eat solid food within a few days.

194.

They have a high metabolic rate and require a diet rich in fiber to support their digestive system.

195.

Degus have been kept as pets for centuries by the indigenous people of Chile.

196.

They were first introduced to the international pet trade in the 1960s and have gained popularity as exotic pets since then.

197.

Degus are not recommended for young children as they have delicate bones and can be easily injured.

198.

They are naturally curious and require mental stimulation and environmental enrichment to prevent boredom.

199.

Degus are susceptible to heatstroke, so it's important to provide them with cool areas and access to fresh water.

200.

They are fascinating creatures with unique behaviors and adaptations, making them a captivating species to observe and care for.

201.

Pinterest was founded in March 2010 by Ben Silbermann, Paul Sciarra, and Evan Sharp.

202.

The idea for Pinterest came from a desire to create a platform where people could collect and organize things they love and find inspiration.

203.

The site was initially launched as a closed beta and gained popularity through word-of-mouth.

204.

Pinterest's early user base consisted mainly of women, with topics like fashion, home decor, and recipes being popular.

205.

The name "Pinterest" is a combination of the words "pin" and "interest," reflecting the concept of pinning or saving items of interest on virtual boards.

206.

In 2011, Pinterest received a major investment from venture capitalists, leading to significant growth and expansion.

207.

The platform officially opened to the public in August 2012, allowing anyone to join and create an account.

208.

Pinterest quickly gained traction and became one of the fastest-growing social media platforms in history.

209.

By 2013, Pinterest had reached 70 million users worldwide.

210.

The visual nature of Pinterest, with its emphasis on images and videos, set it apart from other social media platforms at the time.

211.

Pinterest introduced the concept of "pins" and "boards," where users could save and organize content based on their interests.

212.

In 2014, Pinterest launched its advertising platform, allowing businesses to promote their products and services to users.

213.

The platform continued to innovate, introducing features like buyable pins, which allowed users to make purchases directly within the app.

214.

Pinterest's international expansion started in 2013, with the platform becoming available in multiple languages and countries.

215.

In 2017, Pinterest reached 200 million monthly active users globally.

216.

Pinterest has been praised for its positive and uplifting content, with a focus on inspiration, creativity, and self-improvement.

217.

The platform has become a valuable tool for businesses and content creators to showcase their products and ideas.

218.

Pinterest's algorithm-driven feed and personalized recommendations make it easy for users to discover new content based on their interests.

219.

The company has made efforts to foster a diverse and inclusive community, promoting content that celebrates different cultures, backgrounds, and perspectives.

220.

In 2019, Pinterest became a publicly traded company with its initial public offering (IPO) on the New York Stock Exchange.

221.

Pinterest has expanded beyond its initial focus on lifestyle and home-related content, with categories like travel, fitness, and technology gaining popularity.

222.

The platform has evolved into a valuable search engine, with users often turning to Pinterest for ideas and inspiration.

223.

Pinterest has a strong influence on consumer behavior, with many users actively using the platform to research products before making purchases.

224.

The company has implemented various measures to protect user privacy and combat misinformation on the platform.

225.

Pinterest has also focused on sustainability initiatives, promoting eco-friendly ideas and content related to conservation and reducing waste.

226.

The platform has been used for various social causes, such as spreading awareness about mental health, body positivity, and social justice issues.

227.

Pinterest has collaborated with notable brands and influencers, hosting curated content and partnerships to engage users.

228.

The company has acquired several startups and technologies to enhance its platform and improve user experience.

229.

In recent years, Pinterest has introduced features like Story Pins, which allow users to share interactive and immersive content.

230.

Pinterest has a strong international presence, with users and offices in countries around the world.

231.

The platform has been recognized with numerous awards and accolades for its innovation and user experience.

232.

Pinterest has actively worked to combat the spread of harmful content and misinformation, implementing stricter policies and guidelines.

233.

The company has a strong focus on user engagement and retention, constantly refining its algorithms and features to enhance the user experience.

234.

Pinterest has been praised for its user-friendly interface and intuitive design, making it easy for users to navigate and discover content.

235.

The platform has a robust analytics and insights system, allowing businesses and content creators to track the performance of their pins and boards.

236.

Pinterest has expanded its advertising capabilities over the years, offering a variety of ad formats and targeting options for marketers.

237.

The company has a developer platform that allows third-party apps and services to integrate with Pinterest and enhance the user experience.

238.

Pinterest has launched initiatives to support small businesses, providing resources and tools for entrepreneurs to showcase their products and reach a wider audience.

239.

The company has a strong commitment to user safety, actively combating harassment and inappropriate content through reporting and moderation systems.

240.

Pinterest has a dedicated team of engineers and data scientists working on machine learning and artificial intelligence to improve its recommendation algorithms.

241.

The platform has introduced features like "Tried It" and "Shop the Look," allowing users to see real-life examples and purchase products they discover on Pinterest.

242.

Pinterest has collaborated with publishers and media outlets to create curated content, including recipe ideas, DIY projects, and fashion inspiration.

243.

The platform has launched initiatives to support creators, including the Pinterest Creators Fund, which provides financial assistance to content creators.

244.

Pinterest has partnered with organizations and initiatives focused on social impact, such as promoting mental health resources and supporting underrepresented communities.

245.

The company has a strong commitment to accessibility, continually improving the platform's features and usability for users with disabilities.

246.

Pinterest has expanded into augmented reality (AR), allowing users to virtually try on products and see how they would look in their homes.

247.

The company has actively engaged with its user community, soliciting feedback and suggestions for platform improvements.

248.

Pinterest has a blog and resource center where it shares insights, trends, and best practices for users and businesses.

249.

The company has invested in machine vision technology, enabling users to search for visually similar items and find inspiration from specific elements of images.

250.

Pinterest continues to evolve and adapt to changing user needs and preferences, remaining a popular platform for discovering and saving ideas across various interests and industries.

251.

Logitech was founded in 1981 in Apples, Switzerland by Daniel Borel, Pierluigi Zappacosta, and Giacomo Marini.

252.

The company's initial focus was on computer mice, becoming one of the first manufacturers to produce a commercially successful mouse.

253.

Logitech's first product, the P4 Mouse, was introduced in 1982 and became popular due to its ergonomic design and reliable performance.

254.

In 1983, Logitech expanded its product line to include keyboards, becoming one of the early pioneers in computer input devices.

255.

Logitech was one of the first companies to introduce wireless computer peripherals, launching its first wireless mouse in 1991.

256.

The company's logo, a stylized "L" representing a computer mouse, was designed by designer Stanley Wong in 1987.

257.

Logitech has been at the forefront of innovation in gaming peripherals, developing specialized keyboards, mice, and headsets for gamers.

258.

In 1998, Logitech introduced the Harmony Remote, a universal remote control that revolutionized home entertainment systems by simplifying device control.

259.

Logitech expanded its product range to include webcams, speakers, headphones, and other audio devices in the early 2000s.

260.

The acquisition of Labtec in 2001 allowed Logitech to expand its presence in the audio market.

261.

Logitech has a strong focus on sustainability and environmental responsibility, implementing recycling programs and reducing its carbon footprint.

262.

The company has won numerous awards for its product design, including multiple Red Dot Design Awards and iF Design Awards.

263.

Logitech has a significant presence in the video conferencing market, offering solutions for businesses and individuals.

264.

The company's acquisition of QuickCam in 1998 marked its entry into the webcam market, leading to the development of high-quality video communication devices.

265.

Logitech has a wide range of partnerships with other technology companies, including collaborations with Microsoft, Google, and Apple.

266.

In 2008, Logitech introduced the "Unifying Receiver," a small USB receiver that can connect multiple compatible devices simultaneously.

267.

Logitech has a strong commitment to user experience, conducting extensive research and user testing to optimize its product design and functionality.

268.

The company has developed several proprietary technologies, such as the "Darkfield Laser Tracking" technology for precise tracking on various surfaces.

269.

Logitech's products are known for their durability and longevity, with many users reporting years of reliable performance.

270.

The acquisition of Ultimate Ears in 2008 allowed Logitech to enter the premium audio market, offering high-end headphones and speakers.

271.

Logitech has a global presence, with offices and manufacturing facilities in multiple countries worldwide.

272.

The company has a strong online presence, with an e-commerce platform and partnerships with major online retailers.

273.

Logitech has a dedicated gaming brand called "Logitech G," offering a range of gaming peripherals designed specifically for gamers.

274.

In 2021, Logitech acquired Streamlabs, a popular live streaming software company, to expand its presence in the streaming and content creation market.

275.

Logitech has a strong commitment to corporate social responsibility, supporting various philanthropic initiatives and community outreach programs.

276.

The company's products are used by professionals in various industries, including design, music production, and healthcare.

277.

Logitech has a history of supporting esports and competitive gaming, sponsoring teams and events worldwide.

278.

The company has a diverse product portfolio, catering to different user preferences and needs across various demographics.

279.

Logitech has been recognized for its workplace culture and employee satisfaction, consistently ranking in "Best Places to Work" lists.

280.

The company has a strong focus on accessibility, ensuring that its products are usable and inclusive for individuals with disabilities.

281.

Logitech has a dedicated software ecosystem, including configuration software and drivers, to enhance the user experience and customize device settings.

282.

The acquisition of Slim Devices in 2006 allowed Logitech to enter the network music player market, offering wireless audio streaming solutions.

283.

Logitech has been listed on the Swiss Stock Exchange and the Nasdaq stock exchange, demonstrating its financial stability and growth.

284.

The company's manufacturing processes adhere to strict quality control standards, ensuring the reliability and performance of its products.

285.

Logitech has a history of supporting educational initiatives, providing technology and resources to schools and educational institutions.

286.

The company has won multiple innovation awards for its products, recognizing its contributions to the technology industry.

287.

Logitech's products are compatible with multiple operating systems, including Windows, macOS, and various Linux distributions.

288.

The company's customer support is highly regarded, offering prompt assistance and troubleshooting for users.

289.

Logitech has been an active participant in industry events and trade shows, showcasing its latest products and technologies.

290.

The company has a strong online community, with forums and user groups where customers can connect and share their experiences.

291.

Logitech has made significant advancements in wireless technology, developing efficient and reliable wireless connectivity for its devices.

292.

The company has a commitment to reducing electronic waste, offering recycling programs for its products.

293.

Logitech has been recognized for its design approach, balancing aesthetics and functionality in its product designs.

294.

The company has a history of supporting environmental conservation initiatives, partnering with organizations dedicated to preserving nature.

295.

Logitech has a dedicated research and development team, constantly exploring new technologies and innovations.

296.

The company has a strong focus on ergonomics, designing its products to promote comfort and reduce the risk of repetitive strain injuries.

297.

Logitech has received numerous industry accolades, including CES Innovation Awards and iF Design Awards.

298.

The company's product packaging follows sustainable practices, using recyclable materials and minimizing waste.

299.

Logitech has a commitment to privacy and data security, implementing measures to protect user information.

300.

The company continues to innovate and expand its product range, adapting to the evolving needs and preferences of consumers in the digital age.

301.

Los Cerritos Ranch House is located in Long Beach, California, and is a historic adobe home.

302.

The ranch house was built in 1844 by John Temple, a prominent early Californian landowner and businessman.

303.

The house is a prime example of Monterey Colonial architecture, which combines Spanish and New England architectural styles.

304.

Los Cerritos Ranch House is designated as a National Historic Landmark and is listed on the National Register of Historic Places.

305.

The ranch house sits on a 27-acre site that includes gardens, orchards, and original outbuildings.

306.

The house was originally part of a 27,000-acre ranch that was one of the largest land grants in California.

307.

The ranch house served as the headquarters for the cattle and sheep ranching operations of John Temple and later, his son-in-law, Flint Bixby.

308.

The ranch house has been preserved to reflect the period between 1866 and 1884, showcasing the lifestyle of the Victorian era.

309.

Los Cerritos Ranch House is open to the public and offers guided tours, educational programs, and special events.

310.

The interior of the house features period furnishings and artifacts, giving visitors a glimpse into the daily life of the ranch's inhabitants.

311.

The ranch house includes a parlor, bedrooms, dining room, and kitchen, all furnished in a style reminiscent of the late 19th century.

312.

The surrounding gardens and landscape at Los Cerritos Ranch House feature a variety of native plants and trees.

313.

The site also includes a historic adobe winery building, which is one of the few surviving adobe wineries in California.

314.

Los Cerritos Ranch House is managed by the Los Cerritos Ranch House Foundation, a nonprofit organization dedicated to its preservation and interpretation.

315.

The house has been used as a filming location for movies and television shows, including "The Big Valley" and "The Bold and the Beautiful."

316.

The ranch house provides a unique opportunity to learn about the history of the region and the challenges faced by early California settlers.

317.

The property offers panoramic views of the surrounding landscape, including the nearby San Gabriel Mountains.

318.

Los Cerritos Ranch House has been recognized for its architectural significance and historical importance.

319.

The site hosts special events throughout the year, such as Victorian-era holiday celebrations and living history demonstrations.

320.

The ranch house is known for its well-preserved adobe construction, showcasing the traditional building techniques of the era.

321.

The house has undergone restoration efforts to preserve its original features and ensure its long-term sustainability.

322.

The ranch house is an important cultural and educational resource in the community, offering programs for students and researchers.

323.

The property has been recognized for its historical significance by organizations such as the California State Parks Foundation.

324.

Los Cerritos Ranch House provides a glimpse into the agricultural practices and lifestyles of early Californians.

325.

The site has a visitor center where guests can learn more about the history of the house and its inhabitants.

326.

The ranch house has a storied past, with connections to influential figures in California history, including the Bixby family.

327.

The house is situated in a tranquil setting, surrounded by open space and nature.

328.

Los Cerritos Ranch House offers a unique opportunity to experience the architecture and lifestyle of the mid-19th century.

329.

The property has been meticulously maintained to ensure an authentic and immersive visitor experience.

330.

The ranch house has served as a backdrop for photo shoots, weddings, and other special occasions.

331.

The site hosts educational programs for schools, providing students with hands-on learning opportunities.

332.

Los Cerritos Ranch House has a dedicated team of staff and volunteers who are passionate about preserving its history.

333.

The property has been featured in architectural publications and travel guides as a notable example of early Californian architecture.

334.

The ranch house has been used as a setting for historical reenactments and period-themed events.

335.

The gardens surrounding the house feature a variety of plants and flowers that would have been common during the Victorian era.

336.

The ranch house has been recognized for its architectural details, including its wraparound porch and adobe construction.

337.

The property offers ample parking and accessibility options for visitors with disabilities.

338.

Los Cerritos Ranch House provides a peaceful retreat from the bustling city, allowing visitors to step back in time and connect with history.

339.

The house has been featured in documentaries and television programs exploring the history and culture of California.

340.

The site offers interpretive exhibits and displays that delve into the history of the house, its occupants, and the surrounding area.

341.

Los Cerritos Ranch House has a gift shop where visitors can purchase souvenirs and educational materials.

342.

The ranch house has been a source of inspiration for artists and writers, capturing the essence of a bygone era.

343.

The property has picnic areas and outdoor seating, allowing visitors to relax and enjoy the beautiful surroundings.

344.

Los Cerritos Ranch House is a popular destination for history enthusiasts, architecture buffs, and nature lovers.

345.

The site is easily accessible by car and is located near other historical landmarks and attractions.

346.

The house has been featured in architectural tours and heritage walks, showcasing its significance in the region.

347.

The ranch house has been featured in books and publications exploring the history and heritage of Southern California.

348.

Los Cerritos Ranch House offers guided tours led by knowledgeable docents who provide fascinating insights into the house's history.

349.

The property has been recognized for its efforts in environmental sustainability, implementing practices to conserve water and energy.

350.

Los Cerritos Ranch House continues to be an important cultural and historical landmark, preserving the heritage of early California settlers and sharing their stories with future generations.

351.

Lower Klamath National Wildlife Refuge (NWR) is located in northern California and southern Oregon, covering an area of over 46,900 acres.

352.

Established in 1908, it is the first national wildlife refuge in the United States.

353.

The refuge was established by President Theodore Roosevelt to protect and provide habitat for migratory birds.

354.

Lower Klamath NWR is part of the Klamath Basin National Wildlife Refuge Complex, which includes six other wildlife refuges in the region.

355.

The refuge is situated along the Pacific Flyway, a major migratory bird route stretching from Alaska to South America.

356.

It provides critical habitat for over 200 bird species, including waterfowl, raptors, shorebirds, and songbirds.

357.

Lower Klamath NWR is known for its large population of wintering bald eagles, with up to 100 eagles observed during peak season.

358.

The refuge also supports several endangered and threatened species, such as the California condor and the Yreka phlox.

359.

The diverse habitats within the refuge include marshes, wetlands, open water, grasslands, and forests, providing a rich ecological setting.

360.

The refuge is home to a wide variety of wildlife, including deer, elk, otters, beavers, coyotes, and muskrats.

361.

It offers excellent opportunities for birdwatching, with numerous observation points and a designated auto tour route.

362.

Lower Klamath NWR is a popular destination for hunters, providing opportunities for waterfowl hunting in designated areas.

363.

The refuge has several walking trails and a wildlife viewing platform that allows visitors to observe wildlife in their natural habitats.

364.

It offers photography opportunities, especially during sunrise and sunset when the light enhances the beauty of the landscape and bird activity.

365.

Lower Klamath NWR has a visitor center that provides information about the refuge's history, wildlife, and conservation efforts.

366.

The refuge conducts regular wildlife surveys and research to monitor bird populations and ecosystem health.

367.

It plays a vital role in water management and wetland restoration, working with partners to ensure a sustainable water supply for wildlife.

368.

The refuge collaborates with local Native American tribes to preserve cultural heritage and maintain traditional practices.

369.

Lower Klamath NWR has implemented habitat management strategies, including controlled burns and invasive species removal, to maintain a healthy ecosystem.

370.

The refuge offers environmental education programs for schools and community groups, promoting awareness and appreciation for nature.

371.

It participates in the Junior Duck Stamp Program, encouraging youth to learn about conservation and express their creativity through art.

372.

Lower Klamath NWR is part of the larger Klamath Basin ecosystem, which supports a high level of biodiversity and ecological significance.

373.

The refuge provides critical stopover habitat for migratory birds, allowing them to rest and refuel during their long journeys.

374.

It has designated areas for bird nesting and breeding, contributing to the conservation of threatened bird species.

375.

Lower Klamath NWR has faced challenges such as drought, habitat loss, and water management conflicts, necessitating adaptive management approaches.

376.

The refuge has implemented water conservation measures, including the creation of water control structures and wetland enhancements.

377.

It is a haven for bird photographers, who can capture stunning images of birds in flight, feeding, and engaging in courtship displays.

378.

Lower Klamath NWR hosts annual bird festivals and events, attracting bird enthusiasts and nature lovers from across the country.

379.

The refuge offers opportunities for fishing, boating, and kayaking in designated areas, allowing visitors to explore the waterways.

380.

It has a network of bird blinds and observation decks strategically placed to provide optimal viewing opportunities.

381.

Lower Klamath NWR is recognized as a Globally Important Bird Area by the American Bird Conservancy.

382.

The refuge has a diverse plant community, including cattails, tule reeds, willows, and various wetland vegetation.

383.

It provides habitat for several amphibians, including the Pacific tree frog and the western toad.

384.

Lower Klamath NWR is part of the larger conservation efforts in the Klamath Basin to balance water needs for wildlife and agriculture.

385.

The refuge's wetlands act as natural filters, helping to improve water quality and mitigate the impacts of pollution.

386.

It has an active prescribed burning program to maintain the health and productivity of the grasslands and wetlands.

387.

The refuge offers hunting and fishing workshops to educate participants about responsible and ethical outdoor practices.

388.

Lower Klamath NWR has a designated scenic drive that allows visitors to experience the beauty of the refuge at their own pace.

389.

The refuge is open year-round, although specific areas may have seasonal closures to protect wildlife during critical periods.

390.

It is managed by the U.S. Fish and Wildlife Service, which works closely with local stakeholders and conservation organizations.

391.

Lower Klamath NWR has been recognized for its conservation efforts and received awards for its habitat restoration and wildlife management practices.

392.

The refuge has an active volunteer program, providing opportunities for individuals to contribute to conservation and assist with visitor services.

393.

It has interpretive signage and educational displays throughout the refuge, offering insights into the area's natural and cultural history.

394.

The refuge participates in citizen science programs, encouraging visitors to contribute their observations and data to scientific research.

395.

Lower Klamath NWR has designated photography blinds, providing photographers with unobstructed views of wildlife without causing disturbance.

396.

The refuge collaborates with neighboring wildlife refuges and landowners to create a larger network of protected habitats.

397.

It has partnerships with educational institutions and research organizations to conduct studies on bird migration patterns and wetland ecology.

398.

Lower Klamath NWR has visitor amenities such as restrooms, picnic areas, and a visitor information center.

399.

The refuge's conservation efforts contribute to the overall health of the Klamath River watershed, benefiting both wildlife and local communities.

400.

It offers a serene and tranquil setting for nature enthusiasts, allowing them to disconnect from the fast-paced world and reconnect with the beauty of the natural environment.

401.

Dik-diks are small antelopes native to Eastern and Southern Africa.

402.

They are known for their petite size, with adults typically weighing between 3-6 kilograms (6.6-13.2 pounds).

403.

Dik-diks are named after the sound they make when alarmed, which resembles the "dik-dik" sound.

404.

There are four recognized species of dik-dik: Kirk's dik-dik, Guenther's dik-dik, Salt's dik-dik, and the Damara dik-dik.

405.

They have a distinctive feature of large, dark eyes positioned on the sides of their head, providing them with a wide field of view.

406.

Dik-diks have elongated snouts, which help cool down the air they breathe in hot environments.

407.

They are primarily herbivores, feeding on leaves, shoots, fruits, and flowers.

408.

Dik-diks have a unique adaptation where they can obtain water from their diet, reducing their reliance on external water sources.

409.

These antelopes are monogamous, forming lifelong pair bonds with their mates.

410.

Male dik-diks have small, straight horns, which they use for territorial defense and competition for mates.

411.

They are territorial animals and mark their territory with secretions from their preorbital glands.

412.

Dik-diks are well adapted to their environment and can tolerate high temperatures and arid conditions.

413.

They have specialized kidneys that allow them to conserve water efficiently.

414.

Dik-diks are mostly active during the early morning and late afternoon, resting in the shade during the hottest parts of the day.

415.

Despite their small size, dik-diks are agile and can reach speeds of up to 42 kilometers per hour (26 miles per hour).

416.

They have a keen sense of hearing and rely on their alertness and quick reactions to evade predators.

417.

Dik-diks have a cryptic coat coloration, blending in with their surroundings to avoid detection.

418.

They are preyed upon by larger predators such as lions, leopards, hyenas, and African wild dogs.

419.

Dik-diks communicate using various vocalizations, including alarm calls and soft whistling sounds.

420.

They have scent glands on their feet, which they use to mark their trails and communicate with other dik-diks.

421.

Female dik-diks have a gestation period of around 5-6 months, after which a single calf is born.

422.

The newborn dik-dik is precocial, able to stand and walk shortly after birth.

423.

Dik-dik calves have a distinctive tuft of hair on their heads, which gradually disappears as they mature.

424.

Family bonds are strong in dik-dik pairs, and they often stay together even after the calf becomes independent.

425.

Dik-diks have a lifespan of around 10-12 years in the wild.

426.

They are known for their exceptional camouflage skills, blending into their surroundings to avoid predation.

427.

Dik-diks have specialized tear ducts that allow them to excrete excess salt from their bodies, helping them cope with their diet and arid environments.

428.

They have a unique dental adaptation called hypsodont teeth, which grow continuously throughout their lives to compensate for the wear caused by their abrasive diet.

429.

Dik-diks are known to form symbiotic relationships with birds called oxpeckers, which help remove parasites from their bodies.

430.

These antelopes have an intricate network of blood vessels in their noses that helps cool down the blood before it reaches their brain.

431.

Dik-diks have a keen sense of smell, which they use to detect predators and locate water sources.

432.

They are selective browsers and can eat a wide variety of plant species, adapting their diet to the available vegetation.

433.

Dik-diks have a unique behavior called "pronking," where they perform high jumps with all four feet off the ground simultaneously, possibly as a means of signaling fitness or playfulness.

434.

In some cultures, dik-diks are considered symbols of fidelity and monogamous love due to their lifelong pair bonds.

435.

Dik-diks are important prey species for large predators and play a vital role in maintaining the ecological balance of their habitats.

436.

They have a complex social structure, with established territories and individual home ranges.

437.

Dik-diks are excellent swimmers and can cross water bodies when necessary.

438.

They have a specialized digestive system that allows them to extract nutrients from fibrous plant material efficiently.

439.

Dik-diks are adaptable animals and can inhabit a range of habitats, including grasslands, savannas, woodlands, and shrublands.

440.

They are known to engage in mutual grooming, where they groom each other's fur to remove parasites and strengthen social bonds.

441.

Dik-diks have large, muscular ears that help dissipate heat and enhance their hearing abilities.

442.

They have a strong maternal instinct, with females fiercely
protecting their young from potential threats.

443.

Dik-diks have a unique way of marking their territory by digging
shallow scrapes in the ground and defecating in them.

444.

They have a soft, velvety fur coat that provides insulation and
protection against harsh weather conditions.

445.

Dik-diks have an excellent sense of taste, enabling them to select
nutritious plant species and avoid toxic ones.

446.

They are known to be curious and inquisitive animals, often
investigating their surroundings and new objects in their
environment.

447.

Dik-diks have a small gland near their eyes that secretes a waxy
substance, which is believed to protect their eyes from dust and
debris.

448.

They are capable of making quick turns and sharp maneuvers while
running, helping them evade predators in their fast-paced
environments.

449.

Dik-diks are important seed dispersers, as they consume fruits and
disperse the undigested seeds in their droppings.

450.

These fascinating antelopes have captivated the interest of wildlife enthusiasts and researchers who continue to study their behavior, ecology, and conservation status to ensure their long-term survival.

451.

Domestic pigs, also known as Sus scrofa domesticus, are descendants of wild boars and are one of the most widely distributed and oldest domesticated animals.

452.

They are highly intelligent animals and are often considered to have the intelligence level of a three-year-old human child.

453.

Pigs are social animals and thrive in groups called sounders, which can consist of several individuals.

454.

They have a strong sense of smell and use their snouts to root and forage for food in the ground.

455.

Domestic pigs come in various sizes, ranging from miniature breeds weighing around 20 pounds to larger breeds weighing several hundred pounds.

456.

Pigs have a keen sense of taste and can distinguish between different flavors, which is why they are sometimes used in truffle hunting.

457.

They have a well-developed sense of touch and enjoy being petted and scratched.

458.

Pigs are excellent swimmers and are known to seek out water to cool themselves during hot weather.

459.

They have a remarkable vocal range and can produce a wide variety of sounds, including grunts, squeals, and even barks.

460.

Pigs are omnivores and have a diverse diet that includes grains, fruits, vegetables, insects, and even small animals.

461.

Domestic pigs have a complex digestive system consisting of a large stomach divided into compartments, allowing them to efficiently digest fibrous plant materials.

462.

They have a relatively long lifespan, with some individuals living up to 15 years or more.

463.

Pigs are highly adaptable and can thrive in a variety of environments, from farms to forests.

464.

Domestic pigs have been bred for various purposes, including meat production, as pets, for medical research, and for truffle cultivation.

465.

Pigs have a layer of subcutaneous fat, which helps regulate their body temperature and provides insulation during colder months.

466.

They are known for their high reproductive potential, with sows (female pigs) being capable of giving birth to litters of up to 12 piglets.

467.

Pigs are considered to be clean animals and will establish separate areas for sleeping, eating, and eliminating waste.

468.

Piglets are born with sharp teeth and strong instincts for nursing, usually within a few hours of birth.

469.

Pigs are highly trainable and can learn a variety of tricks and commands.

470.

They have an excellent memory and can remember locations, routines, and even specific individuals.

471.

Pigs have a strong maternal instinct, with sows exhibiting dedicated care towards their piglets.

472.

Pigs have a unique behavior known as "wallowing," where they roll in mud or water to cool down and protect their skin from sunburn and insects.

473.

Pigs have a thick skin, which is why they are relatively resistant to injuries and diseases.

474.

They are naturally curious animals and will investigate their surroundings, often using their snouts to root and explore.

475.

Pigs have an acute sense of hearing and can detect sounds in a wide range of frequencies.

476.

They have an excellent sense of direction and can find their way back home even when transported long distances.

477.

Pigs have a specialized digestive system that allows them to efficiently convert plant material into energy.

478.

Domestic pigs come in a wide variety of colors and patterns, including black, white, brown, and spotted.

479.

Pigs have a thick, bristly coat that protects them from the elements.

480.

They are highly adaptable to different climates and can tolerate both hot and cold weather conditions.

481.

Pigs have a natural inclination to explore and forage, which is why they require ample space and enrichment in their living environment.

482.

Domestic pigs are often used in scientific research due to their physiological similarities to humans.

483.

Pigs have been depicted in various cultures and mythologies, symbolizing different qualities such as fertility, prosperity, and intelligence.

484.

They have a hierarchical social structure within their groups, with dominant individuals asserting their authority over subordinate ones.

485.

Pigs have a well-developed sense of smell, which makes them excellent at detecting truffles, a type of edible fungus highly prized in the culinary world.

486.

They have an excellent sense of balance and coordination, allowing them to navigate uneven terrain and obstacles.

487.

Pigs have a relatively short gestation period of around 114 days, after which the sow gives birth to a litter of piglets.

488.

Domestic pigs have been selectively bred for specific traits, resulting in a wide variety of breeds with distinct characteristics.

489.

They have a layer of fat under their skin, which gives them a rounded appearance.

490.

Pigs are known for their ability to communicate with each other through various vocalizations and body language.

491.

They have a strong sense of social hierarchy and will establish dominance through behaviors like head-butting and pushing.

492.

Pigs have an excellent sense of spatial awareness, which allows them to navigate through narrow spaces and openings.

493.

Domestic pigs have been used in therapy programs for their calming and comforting presence.

494.

Pigs have a highly developed sense of smell, allowing them to detect food sources from long distances.

495.

They have a well-developed sense of touch, with sensitive snouts that help them locate food buried in the ground.

496.

Pigs have a relatively long snout, which is used for rooting, exploring, and digging.

497.

Domestic pigs have been depicted in literature, movies, and popular culture, often portrayed as intelligent and endearing characters.

498.

Pigs have a strong sense of self-preservation and will avoid situations they perceive as dangerous.

499.

They have a unique vocalization known as the "scream," which is emitted when they are stressed, in pain, or frightened.

500.

Pigs have been domesticated for thousands of years and continue to be an important livestock animal worldwide, providing meat, leather, and other valuable resources.

501.

The Ritz-Carlton Hotel Company was founded in 1983, but its origins can be traced back to the early 20th century.

502.

The first Ritz-Carlton hotel, named The Ritz-Carlton, Boston, opened its doors on May 19, 1927.

503.

The hotel was developed by Albert Keller and Swiss hotelier César Ritz, known for his impeccable service standards.

504.

The Ritz-Carlton, Boston quickly became known for its luxurious accommodations and exceptional service, setting a new standard in the hospitality industry.

505.

The Ritz-Carlton expanded to other major cities in the United States, including New York, Philadelphia, and Washington, D.C.

506.

During the Great Depression in the 1930s, The Ritz-Carlton, Boston faced financial difficulties and was eventually sold.

507.

The Ritz-Carlton brand was revitalized in the 1980s when William B. Johnson acquired the rights to the name and established The Ritz-Carlton Hotel Company.

508.

Under Johnson's leadership, The Ritz-Carlton became known for its commitment to personalized service and attention to detail.

509.

In 1995, Marriott International purchased The Ritz-Carlton Hotel Company, forming a strategic partnership to expand the brand globally.

510.

The Ritz-Carlton has since grown into a worldwide luxury hotel chain, with properties in over 30 countries and territories.

511.

The company operates under the motto "We are Ladies and Gentlemen serving Ladies and Gentlemen," emphasizing the importance of exceptional service.

512.

The Ritz-Carlton is renowned for its elegant and opulent hotel designs, often incorporating elements of local culture and heritage.

513.

Each Ritz-Carlton hotel offers luxurious amenities, including spacious guest rooms, upscale dining options, and world-class spa facilities.

514.

The company places a strong emphasis on employee training and empowerment, aiming to create a culture of excellence and professionalism.

515.

The Ritz-Carlton is known for its "Gold Standards," a set of service values and principles that guide every interaction with guests.

516.

The brand has received numerous accolades and awards for its exceptional service and hospitality, including the prestigious Forbes Travel Guide Five-Star rating.

517.

The Ritz-Carlton expanded its portfolio to include luxury residences and resorts, providing guests with extended stays and vacation experiences.

518.

The Ritz-Carlton Reserve is an exclusive collection of resorts located in breathtaking natural settings, offering a secluded and immersive experience.

519.

The company launched The Ritz-Carlton Yacht Collection, an ultra-luxury cruising experience aboard small luxury yachts, providing a unique way to explore the world.

520.

The Ritz-Carlton has a strong commitment to environmental sustainability and social responsibility, implementing various initiatives to reduce its environmental impact.

521.

The brand is involved in numerous philanthropic endeavors, including supporting community projects and partnering with charitable organizations.

522.

The Ritz-Carlton has hosted notable guests, including celebrities, world leaders, and royalty, further enhancing its reputation for exclusivity and prestige.

523.

The Ritz-Carlton has been featured in popular culture, appearing in films, television shows, and novels, cementing its status as a symbol of luxury and sophistication.

524.

The company's dedication to providing exceptional guest experiences has earned it a loyal customer base, with many guests becoming repeat visitors.

525.

The Ritz-Carlton has embraced technology to enhance the guest experience, implementing digital innovations such as mobile check-in, virtual concierge services, and personalized guest preferences.

526.

The brand has a strong focus on culinary excellence, with renowned chefs creating innovative and delectable dining experiences within each hotel.

527.

The Ritz-Carlton has been recognized for its commitment to diversity and inclusion, fostering a welcoming and inclusive environment for guests and employees.

528.

The Ritz-Carlton Leadership Center offers training and consulting services to organizations outside the hospitality industry, sharing its expertise in service excellence and customer engagement.

529.

The Ritz-Carlton continues to expand its global presence, with new hotel openings and planned developments in emerging markets and iconic destinations.

530.

The brand has established partnerships with luxury brands and organizations to offer exclusive experiences and benefits to its guests.

531.

The Ritz-Carlton has been a pioneer in introducing eco-friendly practices in the luxury hotel industry, incorporating energy-saving technologies and sustainable materials into its properties.

532.

The Ritz-Carlton is renowned for its commitment to craftsmanship and attention to detail, with interior designs showcasing exquisite artwork, furniture, and decor.

533.

The Ritz-Carlton has a strong corporate culture that promotes teamwork, integrity, and a passion for service excellence.

534.

The company is actively involved in employee training and development programs, nurturing talent and encouraging career growth within the organization.

535.

The Ritz-Carlton has received numerous accolades for its commitment to employee satisfaction, consistently ranking as one of the best companies to work for in the hospitality industry.

536.

The brand's loyalty program, The Ritz-Carlton Rewards, offers exclusive benefits and privileges to frequent guests, further enhancing the guest experience.

537.

The Ritz-Carlton has a robust commitment to environmental stewardship, implementing sustainable practices in energy management, waste reduction, and water conservation.

538.

The brand has a strong presence in the luxury wedding and event market, offering exquisite venues and personalized services for memorable celebrations.

539.

The Ritz-Carlton has a history of supporting local communities through charitable initiatives and volunteer programs, making a positive impact beyond its hotel properties.

540.

The Ritz-Carlton is known for its iconic lion logo, symbolizing strength, elegance, and a commitment to excellence.

541.

The brand has a dedicated team of artisans and craftsmen who create custom furnishings and artwork for each hotel, ensuring a unique and luxurious ambiance.

542.

The Ritz-Carlton properties are often located in prime destinations, offering breathtaking views of city skylines, pristine beaches, or picturesque landscapes.

543.

The Ritz-Carlton has been recognized for its commitment to accessibility, providing accommodations and services for guests with disabilities.

544.

The brand has implemented rigorous health and safety protocols, especially in response to the COVID-19 pandemic, to ensure the well-being of guests and employees.

545.

The Ritz-Carlton offers immersive and authentic local experiences through its "Ritz-Carlton Memories" program, allowing guests to explore the culture and traditions of their destinations.

546.

The brand has collaborated with renowned designers, architects, and artists to create visually stunning hotel spaces that blend modern luxury with timeless elegance.

547.

The Ritz-Carlton has a long-standing tradition of hosting extravagant galas, charity events, and cultural celebrations, attracting high-profile guests and philanthropists.

548.

The company has a strong commitment to supporting sustainable agriculture and local food sourcing, partnering with local farmers and producers to offer fresh and seasonal ingredients.

549.

The Ritz-Carlton has a rich legacy of hospitality, carrying forward the traditions and values established by its founders while adapting to the evolving needs and preferences of modern travelers.

550.

The brand continues to be a symbol of luxury and refinement, providing guests with unforgettable experiences and exceptional service in some of the world's most desirable locations.

551.

Shopify was founded in 2006 by Tobias Lütke, Daniel Weinand, and Scott Lake.

552.

The idea for Shopify came about when Lütke, an entrepreneur himself, couldn't find a suitable platform to sell snowboards online.

553.

Originally, Shopify was intended to be an online snowboard shop, but the founders quickly realized the potential of their e-commerce platform and shifted their focus.

554.

The first version of Shopify was developed in just a few months, and it officially launched in June 2006.

555.

The early years of Shopify were challenging, with the founders working long hours and personally handling customer support to ensure the success of the platform.

556.

In 2008, Shopify introduced its App Store, allowing third-party developers to create and sell applications that extend the functionality of the platform.

557.

The App Store played a crucial role in the growth of Shopify, as it provided merchants with a wide range of tools and features to enhance their online stores.

558.

In 2009, Shopify raised its first round of funding, securing $7 million in a Series A investment.

559.

The platform gained popularity among small and medium-sized businesses, offering them an accessible and user-friendly solution to sell products online.

560.

Shopify went public in 2015, listing on both the New York Stock Exchange (NYSE) and the Toronto Stock Exchange (TSX) under the ticker symbol "SHOP."

561.

The initial public offering (IPO) raised $131 million and marked a significant milestone in the company's history.

562.

Over the years, Shopify has expanded its product offerings to cater to different types of businesses, including Shopify Plus for enterprise-level merchants and Shopify POS for in-person retail.

563.

In 2017, Shopify launched its own payment processing service called Shopify Payments, allowing merchants to accept credit card payments directly on their online stores.

564.

Shopify has a strong focus on mobile commerce and provides mobile apps for both merchants and customers, enabling them to manage their stores and make purchases on the go.

565.

The platform has a global presence, supporting merchants from over 175 countries and offering multi-language and multi-currency capabilities.

566.

Shopify has played a significant role in the rise of direct-to-consumer (DTC) brands, empowering entrepreneurs to start their own businesses and sell products directly to consumers.

567.

The company has facilitated the growth of numerous successful brands, including Kylie Cosmetics, Allbirds, Gymshark, and many more.

568.

Shopify has a strong ecosystem of partners, including designers, developers, and marketers, who provide services and solutions to help merchants succeed.

569.

The company organizes an annual conference called Shopify Unite, where partners and developers gather to learn about new features, share insights, and network.

570.

Shopify has made strategic acquisitions to enhance its capabilities and expand its market reach. Notable acquisitions include Oberlo, a dropshipping app, and Tictail, a Swedish e-commerce platform.

571.

During the COVID-19 pandemic, Shopify experienced significant growth as more businesses turned to online sales. The company reported a surge in new store creations and increased revenue.

572.

Shopify offers a wide range of integrations with popular third-party platforms and services, including social media channels, email marketing tools, and shipping providers.

573.

The company has a strong commitment to sustainability and has launched initiatives to reduce its carbon footprint, including offsetting emissions from delivery and investing in renewable energy.

574.

In addition to its core e-commerce platform, Shopify has expanded into other areas, such as Shopify Capital, which provides small business financing, and Shopify Fulfillment Network, a warehousing and shipping service.

575.

Shopify has a vibrant community of merchants who share their experiences, insights, and tips through online forums, webinars, and meetups.

576.

The company regularly releases updates and new features to improve the platform and address the evolving needs of online businesses.

577.

Shopify has a transparent pricing model, with different plans available to accommodate businesses of all sizes. It also offers a 14-day free trial for new users.

578.

The company has received numerous awards and accolades for its innovation, entrepreneurship, and workplace culture.

579.

Shopify has a strong social impact program, supporting various charitable initiatives and organizations through donations and employee volunteering.

580.

The company has a user-friendly interface and provides extensive documentation and support resources to help merchants set up and manage their online stores.

581.

Shopify has a robust security infrastructure in place, ensuring the protection of customer data and secure transactions.

582.

The platform offers customizable themes and templates, allowing merchants to create visually appealing and unique online stores without extensive coding knowledge.

583.

Shopify's "Buy Button" feature enables merchants to sell products on external websites and social media platforms, expanding their reach beyond their online stores.

584.

The company has a dedicated team of experts who provide 24/7 customer support via live chat, email, and phone.

585.

Shopify has a strong emphasis on user feedback and actively incorporates merchant suggestions into its product development process.

586.

The platform integrates with popular accounting software, such as QuickBooks and Xero, simplifying financial management for merchants.

587.

Shopify has a strong presence in the dropshipping industry, offering tools and resources to help entrepreneurs build successful dropshipping businesses.

588.

The company has a comprehensive analytics dashboard that provides merchants with valuable insights into their store performance, sales trends, and customer behavior.

589.

Shopify regularly hosts webinars and educational resources to help merchants optimize their online stores, improve marketing strategies, and increase conversions.

590.

The company has a user-friendly checkout process with multiple payment options, including major credit cards, PayPal, and Apple Pay.

591.

Shopify supports multilingual storefronts, allowing merchants to create localized versions of their stores for different target markets.

592.

The company has a dedicated platform for developers, called Shopify Partners, offering tools and resources for building custom apps and themes.

593.

Shopify has an active community forum where merchants can seek advice, share success stories, and connect with fellow entrepreneurs.

594.

The company provides seamless integrations with popular email marketing platforms, enabling merchants to build and nurture customer relationships through email campaigns.

595.

Shopify has a strong focus on mobile-responsive design, ensuring that online stores look and function well on all types of devices.

596.

The company has a robust system for managing inventory, tracking orders, and handling shipping and fulfillment processes.

597.

Shopify's "Abandoned Cart Recovery" feature automatically sends reminders to customers who leave items in their shopping carts, increasing conversion rates.

598.

The platform offers built-in search engine optimization (SEO) features, helping merchants improve their online visibility and attract organic traffic.

599.

Shopify regularly publishes educational content, including blog articles, guides, and case studies, to help merchants stay updated on industry trends and best practices.

600.

The history of Shopify is characterized by constant innovation, adaptability, and a commitment to empowering entrepreneurs to succeed in the e-commerce landscape.

601.

Manzanar War Relocation Center was one of ten internment camps established by the United States government during World War II to detain Japanese Americans.

602.

The camp was located in the Owens Valley of California, approximately 230 miles northeast of Los Angeles.

603.

TManzanar operated from 1942 to 1945 and held over 10,000 Japanese Americans during its peak population.

604.

The decision to incarcerate Japanese Americans was made following the attack on Pearl Harbor in 1941 and the subsequent declaration of war with Japan.

605.

Manzanar was surrounded by barbed wire fences and guarded by military police to prevent the detainees from leaving.

606.

The living conditions at Manzanar were harsh, with hastily constructed barracks and inadequate facilities for sanitation and healthcare.

607.

Families were forced to live in small, crowded rooms with minimal privacy and no individual cooking or bathing facilities.

608.

Despite the difficult conditions, the detainees at Manzanar established a semblance of community and tried to create a sense of normalcy by forming schools, churches, and recreational activities.

609.

Manzanar had its own high school, elementary school, and adult education classes, providing educational opportunities for the detainees.

610.

The camp had a hospital with limited medical staff and facilities. In more severe cases, detainees had to be transported to outside hospitals for treatment.

611.

The harsh climate of the Owens Valley posed additional challenges, with extreme temperatures, dust storms, and strong winds affecting daily life.

612.

Japanese Americans at Manzanar were subjected to strict rules and regulations, including curfews, restricted movements, and limitations on personal belongings.

613.

Despite the injustices they faced, many detainees at Manzanar demonstrated resilience and resourcefulness by engaging in gardening, arts and crafts, and other creative pursuits.

614.

The Manzanar camp had its own newspaper, called the Manzanar Free Press, which provided information and served as a means of communication within the community.

615.

The detainees faced significant economic hardships, as many lost their homes, businesses, and possessions due to forced relocation.

616.

Manzanar became a center for cultural and artistic expression, with detainees organizing concerts, plays, and art exhibitions to maintain their sense of identity and dignity.

617.

Notable individuals who were interned at Manzanar include artist and activist Miné Okubo, photographer Ansel Adams, and future U.S. Secretary of Transportation Norman Mineta.

618.

Manzanar was the first of the ten internment camps to be designated as a National Historic Site, which occurred in 1992.

619.

The site is now managed by the National Park Service and serves as a reminder of the injustice and hardships endured by Japanese Americans during World War II.

620.

The Manzanar National Historic Site includes reconstructed barracks, a visitor center, a museum, and interpretive exhibits that educate visitors about the experiences of the detainees.

621.

Each year, a pilgrimage takes place at the site, where former detainees, their families, and the public come together to remember and honor the history of Manzanar.

622.

The National Park Service conducts ongoing research and preservation efforts to ensure the historical accuracy and integrity of the Manzanar site.

623.

In 2020, the site celebrated its 50th anniversary as a National Historic Site, marking half a century of preserving and sharing the history of the internment camps.

624.

The experiences of Japanese Americans at Manzanar and other internment camps prompted a reexamination of civil rights and led to the eventual issuance of a formal apology and reparations by the U.S. government in 1988.

625.

Manzanar serves as a poignant reminder of the importance of upholding civil liberties and protecting the rights of all individuals, regardless of their background or ethnicity.

626.

The camp's name, "Manzanar," means "apple orchard" in Spanish, reflecting the agricultural history of the region.

627.

The Manzanar War Relocation Center was designated as a California Historical Landmark in 1972.

628.

The majority of the detainees at Manzanar were American citizens, born and raised in the United States.

629.

Manzanar was one of the largest and most well-known of the internment camps, but it was just one of several similar camps established during World War II.

630.

The decision to incarcerate Japanese Americans was based on racial prejudice and wartime hysteria rather than any evidence of disloyalty or threat to national security.

631.

The internment of Japanese Americans was later recognized as a grave violation of their civil rights and constitutional protections.

632.

The construction of Manzanar was completed in less than four months after the signing of Executive Order 9066, which authorized the internment of Japanese Americans.

633.

Manzanar had its own water supply system, with wells and a water treatment plant to meet the needs of the population.

634.

The detainees at Manzanar were responsible for performing various tasks and jobs within the camp, such as maintenance, farming, and administrative work.

635.

The camp had a small library that provided books, newspapers, and magazines to the detainees, allowing them to continue their education and stay informed about the outside world.

636.

Many detainees at Manzanar participated in organized sports, including baseball, basketball, and sumo wrestling, as a way to stay physically active and maintain a sense of community.

637.

The majority of the detainees were eventually released from the camps after the end of World War II, although some faced challenges reintegrating into society and rebuilding their lives.

638.

Manzanar played a significant role in the redress and reparations movement of the 1980s, which sought recognition and compensation for the injustices endured by Japanese Americans during their internment.

639.

The experiences of Japanese Americans at Manzanar and other internment camps have been documented in various forms of media, including books, films, and oral histories.

640.

The National Park Service offers educational programs and resources for teachers and students to learn about the history of Manzanar and the internment of Japanese Americans.

641.

The Manzanar site is a popular destination for researchers, scholars, and individuals interested in studying the history of internment camps and the experiences of Japanese Americans during World War II.

642.

In 1985, a monument was erected at Manzanar to commemorate the internment of Japanese Americans and serve as a reminder of the importance of preserving civil liberties.

643.

The Manzanar site includes a cemetery where some detainees who died during their internment are buried. The cemetery serves as a solemn reminder of the hardships and losses experienced by the community.

644.

Manzanar has been the subject of numerous art exhibitions, photography projects, and creative works that explore the themes of incarceration, identity, and resilience.

645.

The Manzanar National Historic Site offers guided tours and self-guided walking paths that allow visitors to explore the camp's layout and learn about the daily life of the detainees.

646.

The site has a replica of a guard tower to illustrate the restrictive conditions and constant surveillance experienced by the detainees.

647.

The ongoing preservation efforts at Manzanar aim to maintain the authenticity of the site and ensure that future generations can learn from and reflect upon this significant chapter in American history.

648.

Manzanar has been visited by numerous political leaders, activists, and public figures who recognize the importance of acknowledging and learning from the mistakes of the past.

649.

The history of Manzanar serves as a powerful reminder of the importance of safeguarding civil liberties and promoting social justice in times of crisis.

650.

The stories and experiences of the Japanese American community at Manzanar continue to inspire conversations about human rights, diversity, and the pursuit of a more inclusive society.

651.

Mare Island Naval Shipyard is located in Vallejo, California, on Mare Island in the San Francisco Bay.

652.

It was the first United States Navy base on the West Coast, established in 1854.

653.

Mare Island Naval Shipyard played a crucial role in the development of the U.S. Navy's Pacific Fleet during World War II.

654.

The shipyard covered an area of approximately 5,200 acres and included various facilities such as dry docks, machine shops, foundries, and housing for the workers.

655.

Mare Island was responsible for building and repairing numerous Navy vessels, including battleships, cruisers, submarines, and aircraft carriers.

656.

The USS California, the first modern battleship of the U.S. Navy, was built at Mare Island Naval Shipyard and launched in 1907.

657.

During World War II, the shipyard employed over 50,000 workers, including many women who took on jobs traditionally held by men.

658.

The shipyard was known for its innovation and advanced technology, including the use of prefabricated sections for ship construction.

659.

Mare Island Naval Shipyard was the site of several major modernization projects, including the overhaul and conversion of ships to accommodate new technologies and weaponry.

660.

The shipyard was also involved in nuclear research and development, working on the nuclear propulsion systems for submarines.

661.

The USS Nautilus, the world's first operational nuclear-powered submarine, underwent extensive work and refitting at Mare Island in the 1950s.

662.

Mare Island played a critical role in the development of the Polaris missile program during the Cold War era.

663.

The shipyard faced closure multiple times throughout its history but managed to remain operational until its official closure in 1996.

664.

Over its 142 years of operation, Mare Island Naval Shipyard constructed over 500 vessels, including 17 submarines and eight aircraft carriers.

665.

The shipyard's workforce included skilled craftsmen, engineers, machinists, electricians, and a range of other specialized tradespeople.

666.

Mare Island's location in the San Francisco Bay provided strategic advantages for shipbuilding and maintenance, as well as access to key resources and transportation routes.

667.

The shipyard employed innovative construction methods, including the use of shipways and a floating dry dock to accommodate different types of vessels.

668.

During World War II, the shipyard's workforce achieved remarkable productivity, completing ships in record time to support the war effort.

669.

Mare Island Naval Shipyard was designated as a National Historic Landmark in 1975.

670.

The shipyard's closure in 1996 resulted in the loss of thousands of jobs and had a significant economic impact on the surrounding community.

671.

Mare Island has since undergone redevelopment efforts, with portions of the shipyard repurposed for industrial, commercial, and residential use.

672.

The Mare Island Historic Park Foundation was established to preserve and interpret the shipyard's history, artifacts, and structures.

673.

Several of the historic buildings at Mare Island have been restored and converted into museums, showcasing the shipyard's legacy.

674.

The shipyard's legacy extends beyond its physical structures, as many former workers and their families have fond memories and personal connections to Mare Island.

675.

The Mare Island Naval Cemetery, established in 1856, is the final resting place for over 800 military personnel and their family members.

676.

The cemetery features various memorials, including a monument dedicated to those who lost their lives in the USS Maine explosion in Havana Harbor in 1898.

677.

Mare Island Naval Shipyard was known for its tight-knit community and vibrant social life, with various clubs, organizations, and events for the workers and their families.

678.

The shipyard had its own newspaper, The Mare Island Grapevine, which provided news, updates, and entertainment for the workers.

679.

Mare Island's workforce was diverse, with people from different backgrounds and ethnicities working together to support the Navy's mission.

680.

The shipyard's closure led to the establishment of the Mare Island Heritage Trust, which focuses on preserving and interpreting the island's natural and cultural resources.

681.

Mare Island has been used as a filming location for several movies and TV shows, including "The Pursuit of Happyness" and "MythBusters."

682.

The shipyard's dry docks were among the largest in the world, capable of accommodating large naval vessels for repair and maintenance.

683.

Mare Island was a hub of activity during times of war, with ships constantly coming and going, undergoing repairs, and receiving necessary supplies.

684.

The shipyard had its own fire department, medical facilities, and other support services to ensure the well-being of the workers and the efficient operation of the shipyard.

685.

Mare Island's location near the city of San Francisco made it an important strategic asset for the U.S. Navy's Pacific operations.

686.

The shipyard's closure marked the end of an era for naval shipbuilding on the West Coast, as many of the functions were consolidated at other facilities.

687.

Mare Island played a role in supporting space exploration efforts, including the construction and repair of tracking stations used in the early days of NASA's space missions.

688.

The shipyard was named after Mariano G. Vallejo, a prominent Californian landowner and politician who played a significant role in the state's early history.

689.

Mare Island's workforce was highly skilled, with many workers learning their trades through apprenticeship programs offered by the shipyard.

690.

The shipyard employed a significant number of women during World War II, helping to pave the way for greater gender equality in the workplace.

691.

Mare Island Naval Shipyard was an important economic driver for the Vallejo area, providing employment opportunities and supporting local businesses.

692.

The shipyard's workers were often referred to as "Mare Island Brats," a term of endearment for those who grew up in the shipyard community.

693.

The shipyard faced several challenges throughout its history, including labor disputes, financial constraints, and changing priorities within the Navy.

694.

The Mare Island Naval Shipyard Museum offers visitors a glimpse into the shipyard's history, featuring exhibits on shipbuilding, the workforce, and notable vessels.

695.

The shipyard's impact extended beyond its immediate surroundings, as many of the ships built or repaired at Mare Island played significant roles in U.S. naval operations worldwide.

696.

Mare Island's location in the San Francisco Bay Area attracted skilled workers from various parts of the country, contributing to the shipyard's expertise and diversity.

697.

The shipyard's closure led to the transfer of many of its functions to private contractors, marking a shift in the way naval maintenance and repair work was conducted.

698.

Mare Island Naval Shipyard was known for its strong sense of community and camaraderie among its workers, who often forged lifelong friendships and connections.

699.

The shipyard's legacy is celebrated through various events and reunions, bringing together former workers and their families to reminisce and share stories.

700.

The history of Mare Island Naval Shipyard serves as a reminder of the important role it played in the defense of the nation, the advancement of naval technology, and the lives of the people who called it home.

701.

Dragonflies are ancient insects that have been around for over 300 million years, predating dinosaurs.

702.

There are over 5,000 known species of dragonflies found worldwide.

703.

Dragonflies are excellent flyers and can reach speeds of up to 30 miles per hour (48 kilometers per hour).

704.

They have two pairs of wings that they can move independently, allowing them to perform intricate aerial maneuvers.

705.

Dragonflies have a unique life cycle that includes an aquatic nymph stage and a flying adult stage.

706.

The nymphs are aquatic and live in freshwater bodies such as ponds, lakes, and streams.

707.

Dragonfly nymphs are voracious predators, feeding on small aquatic insects, tadpoles, and even small fish.

708.

Adult dragonflies are also predators and feed on flying insects like mosquitoes, flies, and butterflies.

709.

Dragonflies have large compound eyes that give them excellent vision, allowing them to detect prey and predators with precision.

710.

Their eyes can contain up to 30,000 individual lenses, giving them a wide field of vision.

711.

Dragonflies are known for their vibrant colors and intricate wing patterns, which often serve as a form of camouflage or warning to predators.

712.

They are capable of flying in all six directions: up, down, forward, backward, left, and right.

713.

Dragonflies are territorial creatures and will fiercely defend their chosen hunting grounds.

714.

The lifespan of a dragonfly varies by species, but most adult dragonflies live for several weeks to a few months.

715.

Dragonflies are indicators of freshwater ecosystem health. Their presence in an area is often a sign of clean water and a diverse ecosystem.

716.

Dragonflies are known for their mating behaviors, including impressive aerial acrobatics and elaborate courtship displays.

717.

After mating, female dragonflies lay their eggs in or near water, attaching them to plants or other surfaces.

718.

Dragonfly eggs hatch into nymphs, which spend the majority of their lives underwater before emerging as adults.

719.

Dragonflies are found on every continent except Antarctica.

720.

Dragonflies are excellent hunters and are estimated to catch and consume hundreds of mosquitoes and other insects each day.

721.

Dragonflies are important pollinators, transferring pollen from flower to flower as they feed on nectar.

722.

Dragonflies have a unique ability to regulate their body temperature. They can warm up their flight muscles by basking in the sun and cool down by perching in the shade.

723.

Dragonflies are believed to have one of the best vision systems in the insect world, allowing them to see ultraviolet light and polarized light.

724.

Some dragonfly species are migratory and travel long distances in search of suitable breeding and feeding grounds.

725.

Dragonflies have a specialized organ called the "rectal gills" that allows them to extract oxygen from water during their nymph stage.

726.

Dragonflies are often associated with good luck and are considered symbols of strength, change, and adaptability in many cultures.

727.

In Japan, dragonflies are admired for their beauty and are often depicted in traditional art and literature.

728.

Dragonflies are an important part of food chains and provide a food source for other animals, including birds, fish, and amphibians.

729.

Dragonflies have a unique ability to hover in mid-air, making them highly efficient hunters.

730.

Some dragonflies have incredible camouflage abilities, blending seamlessly into their surroundings to evade predators.

731.

Dragonflies have been used in scientific research to study flight mechanics and biomimicry for designing efficient aerial vehicles.

732.

Dragonflies are known for their exceptional flying skills and can change direction mid-flight with incredible agility.

733.

Dragonflies have a specialized mouthpart called a "labium" that they use to catch and consume prey.

734.

Dragonflies undergo incomplete metamorphosis, meaning they do not have a pupal stage like butterflies and moths.

735.

Dragonflies have a high metabolic rate, allowing them to be active and agile predators.

736.

Dragonflies have been around since the time of the dinosaurs and have survived multiple mass extinction events.

737.

Dragonflies are more closely related to damselflies than they are to other insects like butterflies or bees.

738.

Dragonflies are celebrated in some cultures as symbols of courage, strength, and prosperity.

739.

Dragonflies have been the subject of many myths and folklore, often representing transformation and change.

740.

Dragonflies are incredibly efficient predators, with some species catching prey in mid-air 95% of the time.

741.

Dragonflies have an impressive hunting technique called "hawking," where they patrol their territory and snatch prey out of the air.

742.

Dragonflies have been used as biological control agents to manage populations of pest insects in agricultural settings.

743.

Dragonflies have a unique mating position called the "wheel position," where the male grasps the female behind the head while they fly together.

744.

Dragonflies have been studied for their ability to detect and respond to polarized light, which helps them navigate and locate prey.

745.

Dragonflies have an incredible sense of balance and can adjust their wing movements to compensate for disturbances in flight.

746.

Dragonflies have been observed engaging in territorial disputes, with males defending their territory from intruders.

747.

Dragonflies have been used as indicators of climate change, as shifts in their distribution and behavior can indicate changes in ecosystems.

748.

Dragonflies are excellent fliers, capable of flying up to 60 miles (97 kilometers) in a day during migration.

749.

Dragonflies are often associated with water bodies, but some species can also be found in grasslands, forests, and even deserts.

750.

Dragonflies have captivated human interest for centuries, inspiring art, literature, and scientific research into their fascinating behaviors and adaptations.

751.

Dromedary camels, also known as Arabian camels, are native to the Arabian Peninsula and North Africa.

752.

They are well adapted to desert environments and can withstand extreme temperatures and scarce water resources.

753.

Dromedary camels have a single hump on their back, which stores fat reserves that can be used as an energy source during long journeys without food.

754.

The hump is not used to store water; instead, camels rely on their efficient water conservation mechanisms.

755.

Dromedary camels can go for several days without water, and when they do drink, they can consume up to 30 gallons (113 liters) in one sitting.

756.

They have long, curved necks and powerful legs that help them traverse sandy terrain.

757.

Adult dromedary camels can weigh between 600 and 1,200 kilograms (1,300 to 2,600 pounds).

758.

They have large, tough feet that distribute their weight over the sand and prevent them from sinking.

759.

Dromedary camels have a unique oval-shaped red blood cell that helps maintain blood flow during dehydration.

760.

They have long eyelashes and bushy eyebrows that protect their eyes from sand and harsh desert winds.

761.

Dromedary camels have a split upper lip that allows them to eat thorny desert plants without injuring themselves.

762.

They have a keen sense of smell and can detect water sources from miles away.

763.

Dromedary camels are herbivores and primarily feed on desert vegetation, including grasses, leaves, and thorny bushes.

764.

They are ruminants, meaning they have a specialized digestive system that allows them to regurgitate and re-chew their food for better digestion.

765.

Dromedary camels have been domesticated for thousands of years and have been used as transportation, sources of milk and meat, and companionship.

766.

They have played a significant role in the trade routes of the ancient Silk Road, carrying goods across vast distances.

767.

Dromedary camels have a unique gait called "pacing," where both legs on one side move together, providing a smooth and stable ride for their riders.

768.

They have strong social structures and live in herds led by a dominant male.

769.

Dromedary camels have a gestation period of around 13 months, and females typically give birth to a single calf.

770.

The newborn calf can stand and walk within an hour of birth.

771.

Dromedary camels have a lifespan of around 40 to 50 years.

772.

They have a strong immune system that enables them to resist many diseases and parasites commonly found in desert environments.

773.

Dromedary camels are highly valued by the Bedouin people, who have a deep cultural and historical connection with these animals.

774.

Their milk is nutritious and can be consumed by humans, but it has a slightly salty taste.

775.

Dromedary camels have been used in scientific research to understand their adaptations to arid environments and to develop strategies for water conservation.

776.

They have been introduced to various parts of the world, including Australia and the United States, where they are used for meat production and tourism.

777.

Dromedary camels have been used in camel racing, a popular sport in countries like the United Arab Emirates, Qatar, and Saudi Arabia.

778.

Their long, curved canine teeth, called "fighting teeth," are used for dominance displays and occasionally for combat with other males.

779.

Dromedary camels have a thick fur coat that protects them from the harsh desert sun during the day and keeps them warm in cold desert nights.

780.

They have large, flaring nostrils that can be closed to prevent sand from entering their respiratory system.

781.

Dromedary camels have a specialized kidney structure that allows them to reabsorb water from urine, reducing water loss.

782.

They can tolerate dehydration levels of up to 40% of their body weight.

783.

Dromedary camels have been used in military operations, serving as transport and supply carriers in arid and desert regions.

784.

The dromedary camel is the national animal of Saudi Arabia and appears on the country's coat of arms.

785.

They have been depicted in ancient rock art and carvings, showcasing their significance in human history.

786.

Dromedary camels have been featured in numerous folktales and cultural traditions of the regions where they are found.

787.

They have been recognized as a valuable asset for sustainable desert farming practices, as their dung can be used as fertilizer.

788.

Dromedary camels have adapted to various climatic conditions, including extreme heat and cold.

789.

They are highly intelligent animals and can learn and remember complex tasks.

790.

Dromedary camels have been studied for their unique ability to tolerate high blood glucose levels, which could provide insights into managing diabetes in humans.

791.

Their long legs help distribute their weight over a larger surface area, minimizing sinking in the sand.

792.

Dromedary camels have been used as therapy animals, providing emotional support and companionship to people in need.

793.

They have been known to form strong bonds with their human handlers and can recognize familiar faces and voices.

794.

Dromedary camels are often depicted in Middle Eastern art and literature, symbolizing resilience, endurance, and desert culture.

795.

They have been employed in environmental conservation efforts, as their browsing habits help control invasive plant species in desert ecosystems.

796.

Dromedary camels have a unique ability to metabolize stored fat in their humps, providing a source of energy when food is scarce.

797.

They are skilled swimmers and can traverse bodies of water if necessary.

798.

Dromedary camels have been used in camel beauty pageants, where their appearance, size, and symmetry are judged.

799.

They have been genetically studied to better understand their adaptations and their evolutionary history.

800.

Dromedary camels have become popular tourist attractions, allowing people from around the world to experience riding and interacting with these fascinating creatures.

801.

Crocs, also known as Crocs, Inc., is an American company that specializes in the manufacturing and retailing of casual footwear.

802.

The company was founded in 2002 by Scott Seamans, Lyndon "Duke" Hanson, and George Boedecker Jr.

803.

The original design of Crocs was inspired by a foam clog made by a Canadian company called Foam Creations.

804.

Crocs initially targeted the boating and outdoor recreation market with their slip-resistant and water-friendly shoes.

805.

The first Crocs shoe, known as the Beach model, was introduced in 2002 and gained popularity among boaters and water sports enthusiasts.

806.

Crocs are made from a proprietary closed-cell resin material called Croslite, which provides cushioning, durability, and odor resistance.

807.

The distinctive design of Crocs features a clog-like shape with ventilation holes on the top and sides of the shoe.

808.

Crocs gained widespread recognition in 2006 when they became popular among hospital workers who appreciated their comfort and easy-to-clean properties.

809.

The company experienced rapid growth in the mid-2000s, with sales reaching $847 million in 2007.

810.

In 2006, Crocs went public and became a publicly traded company on the NASDAQ stock exchange.

811.

Crocs expanded its product line beyond the original clogs and introduced various styles, including sandals, sneakers, flats, and boots.

812.

The brand's popularity grew among celebrities and athletes, who were spotted wearing Crocs both casually and in professional settings.

813.

Despite initial success, Crocs faced criticism for their unconventional design and was often labeled as a fashion faux pas.

814.

Crocs responded to the criticism by partnering with designers and celebrities to create limited edition collaborations, boosting their fashion appeal.

815.

The company introduced Jibbitz™, decorative charms that could be inserted into the ventilation holes of Crocs to customize the appearance.

816.

Crocs faced legal challenges regarding patent infringement, particularly from companies producing similar-looking shoes.

817.

The company expanded globally and opened retail stores in major cities around the world.

818.

Crocs launched a children's line called Crocs Kids, featuring smaller sizes and playful designs.

819.

In 2008, Crocs faced a decline in sales and financial challenges due to overexpansion and a decline in consumer demand.

820.

The company implemented cost-cutting measures, including closing manufacturing facilities and reducing its workforce.

821.

Crocs launched a successful marketing campaign called "Come As You Are," emphasizing comfort, versatility, and self-expression.

822.

The company introduced licensed collaborations with popular brands and characters, including Disney, Marvel, and Star Wars.

823.

Crocs expanded its product offerings to include accessories such as bags, hats, and sunglasses.

824.

The brand gained popularity on social media platforms, with fans sharing photos and creative ways to style their Crocs.

825.

Crocs gained attention during the COVID-19 pandemic as healthcare workers praised their comfort and easy sanitization.

826.

The company donated thousands of pairs of shoes to healthcare professionals and launched the "A Free Pair for Healthcare" program.

827.

Crocs collaborated with renowned fashion designers, including Christopher Kane, Balenciaga, and Justin Bieber, to create high-fashion interpretations of their shoes.

828.

In 2020, Crocs reported a record-breaking revenue of $1.38 billion, driven by increased e-commerce sales and strong demand.

829.

The company expanded its sustainability initiatives, including reducing waste, increasing recycled content, and improving manufacturing processes.

830.

Crocs launched a recycling program, allowing customers to return their worn-out shoes for recycling into new products.

831.

The brand's popularity expanded beyond the original clogs, with new styles and collections appealing to a wider audience.

832.

Crocs continued to innovate by introducing new technologies, such as LiteRide™ foam, which offers even more comfort and lightweight cushioning.

833.

The company collaborated with artists and musicians to create limited edition designs, such as the Post Malone x Crocs collaboration, which sold out within minutes.

834.

Crocs partnered with celebrities like Priyanka Chopra Jonas and Bad Bunny, further increasing their cultural relevance.

835.

The company celebrated its 20th anniversary in 2022, marking two decades of providing comfortable and distinctive footwear.

836.

Crocs expanded its presence in the fashion industry by participating in major fashion events and collaborating with influential fashion publications.

837.

The company launched a sustainability initiative called "Crocs Cares" to support various charitable organizations and environmental causes.

838.

Crocs received recognition and awards for its commitment to corporate social responsibility and sustainability practices.

839.

The company's social media presence and engagement grew exponentially, with millions of followers and user-generated content.

840.

Crocs established partnerships with retailers worldwide, expanding their distribution channels and availability.

841.

The brand has been endorsed by athletes, including professional golfers and tennis players who appreciate the comfort and stability of Crocs during their games.

842.

Crocs launched a program called "Crocs Cares Volunteers" to encourage employees to participate in volunteer activities in their local communities.

843.

The company experienced a surge in demand during the "stay-at-home" period of the COVID-19 pandemic, as people sought comfortable footwear for indoor activities.

844.

Crocs created special editions and collections to honor and celebrate cultural events and holidays, such as Pride Month and Chinese New Year.

845.

The brand expanded its offerings to include sustainable materials, such as Crocs made from recycled ocean plastic.

846.

Crocs collaborated with renowned artists and designers to create unique and artistic interpretations of their shoes, blurring the lines between fashion and art.

847.

The company actively engages with its online community, responding to customer feedback and suggestions for new designs and collaborations.

848.

Crocs established a strong presence in the retail market by partnering with major department stores and online platforms.

849.

The company's dedication to comfort, functionality, and self-expression resonates with a diverse customer base of all ages and backgrounds.

850.

Crocs continues to evolve and adapt to changing consumer preferences while staying true to its core values of comfort, innovation, and inclusivity.

851.

Gucci is an Italian luxury fashion brand founded in 1921 by Guccio Gucci.

852.

The brand was initially focused on producing leather goods, specifically luggage and handbags.

853.

Gucci's signature logo, the intertwined double G, was introduced in the 1960s and became an iconic symbol of the brand.

854.

In the 1950s and 1960s, Gucci gained popularity among Hollywood celebrities, further solidifying its reputation as a luxury brand.

855.

The company expanded its product range to include ready-to-wear clothing, shoes, accessories, and fragrances.

856.

Gucci experienced financial challenges in the 1980s due to internal conflicts and counterfeiting issues.

857.

Tom Ford joined Gucci as Creative Director in 1994 and revitalized the brand with his innovative and provocative designs.

858.

Under Tom Ford's leadership, Gucci became known for its bold and sensual aesthetic, which appealed to a younger audience.

859.

Gucci became part of the luxury conglomerate Kering (formerly known as PPR) in 1999.

860.

Alessandro Michele was appointed Creative Director of Gucci in 2015, bringing a new creative vision to the brand.

861.

Alessandro Michele's designs for Gucci are characterized by a romantic, eclectic, and whimsical style, incorporating vintage-inspired elements.

862.

The Gucci Bloom fragrance, launched in 2017, became a bestseller and played a significant role in the brand's revival.

863.

Gucci is renowned for its craftsmanship and attention to detail, with many products featuring intricate embroidery, embellishments, and unique materials.

864.

The brand has collaborated with various artists, including Dapper Dan, a Harlem-based designer known for his custom creations using Gucci fabrics.

865.

Gucci has a strong presence in the luxury fashion industry, with flagship stores in major fashion capitals around the world.

866.

The Gucci Bamboo bag, introduced in 1947, remains an iconic and timeless accessory for the brand.

867.

Gucci's "Flora" print, designed by artist Vittorio Accornero in 1966, has become synonymous with the brand's aesthetic and is still used in many collections.

868.

The Gucci Guilty fragrance, launched in 2010, became one of the brand's most successful fragrance lines.

869.

Gucci has been a pioneer in sustainability efforts in the fashion industry, implementing initiatives to reduce its environmental impact.

870.

The brand has partnered with organizations such as UNICEF to support various social and humanitarian causes.

871.

Gucci has embraced digital innovation, launching immersive digital campaigns and engaging with its audience through social media platforms.

872.

The Gucci "GG Marmont" handbag, introduced in 2016, quickly gained popularity and became a coveted item among fashion enthusiasts.

873.

The Gucci "Ace" sneakers, featuring the iconic green and red Web stripe, have become a staple in the brand's footwear collection.

874.

Gucci has collaborated with renowned filmmakers for its advertising campaigns, including Harmony Korine and Glen Luchford.

875.

The Gucci logo has undergone various redesigns and adaptations over the years, while maintaining its distinctive identity.

876.

Gucci has expanded its product offering to include home décor items, such as cushions, candles, and tableware.

877.

The Gucci "Dionysus" handbag, named after the Greek god of wine and celebration, has become a coveted accessory known for its unique hardware.

878.

Gucci has opened art spaces and exhibitions, such as the Gucci Garden in Florence, showcasing the brand's history and creative collaborations.

879.

The Gucci "Princetown" loafers, featuring a horsebit detail, have gained popularity and have been worn by numerous celebrities and fashion influencers.

880.

Gucci has embraced inclusivity and diversity in its campaigns, featuring models of different ethnicities, body types, and ages.

881.

The brand has launched limited-edition capsule collections in collaboration with influential personalities, such as Gucci x Dapper Dan and Gucci x Disney.

882.

Gucci has been recognized with numerous awards and accolades for its fashion design, innovation, and brand management.

883.

The Gucci "Sylvie" handbag, introduced in 2016, combines classic and contemporary elements, featuring a distinctive chain detail and a web ribbon.

884.

The brand has actively supported emerging artists and designers through initiatives like the Gucci ArtLab and the Gucci Design Fellowship program.

885.

Gucci has a dedicated research and development department, constantly exploring new materials, techniques, and technologies to push the boundaries of fashion design.

886.

The Gucci "Bee" motif, inspired by the House's archives, has become a recognizable symbol in Gucci's collections.

887.

Gucci has embraced the concept of "Guccification," encouraging self-expression and individuality through its designs and campaigns.

888.

The brand has collaborated with renowned photographers, such as Glen Luchford and Petra Collins, to create visually striking advertising campaigns.

889.

Gucci has launched sustainable initiatives, including the "Gucci Equilibrium" platform, which aims to promote social and environmental responsibility.

890.

The Gucci "Ophidia" handbag collection, inspired by vintage luggage, features the brand's iconic GG logo and distinctive striped web detail.

891.

Gucci has participated in major fashion events and shows, such as Milan Fashion Week, where it showcases its latest collections.

892.

The Gucci "Rhyton" sneakers, characterized by their chunky silhouette and bold graphics, have become a popular choice among sneaker enthusiasts.

893.

The brand has collaborated with renowned musicians, such as Elton John and Florence Welch, for special projects and campaigns.

894.

Gucci has a strong commitment to ethical practices, ensuring fair labor conditions and responsible sourcing of materials.

895.

The brand has explored unconventional venues for its fashion shows, including a surgical operating room and an ancient Roman necropolis.

896.

Gucci has established partnerships with influential retailers and e-commerce platforms to expand its global reach.

897.

The Gucci "Marmont" belt, featuring the double G logo as a buckle, has become a sought-after accessory that can elevate any outfit.

898.

Gucci has a dedicated team of artisans who meticulously handcraft many of its products, ensuring the highest level of quality.

899.

The brand has opened pop-up stores and immersive retail experiences in various cities, offering customers a unique and interactive shopping environment.

900.

Gucci continues to push boundaries and challenge conventional fashion norms, remaining a leading force in the luxury fashion industry.

901.

The Marin County Civic Center is located in San Rafael, California, USA.

902.

It was designed by renowned architect Frank Lloyd Wright and completed in 1962.

903.

The Civic Center is known for its unique and futuristic design, with long, low-slung buildings and a distinctive blue roof.

904.

It is considered one of Frank Lloyd Wright's last and largest architectural masterpieces.

905.

The construction of the Civic Center took six years, from 1960 to 1966.

906.

The Civic Center was intended to be a centralized government complex for Marin County.

907.

The complex includes the County Administration Building, Hall of Justice, and the Marin Center, which houses a variety of cultural and performing arts venues.

908.

The central rotunda of the Civic Center serves as the main entrance and features a striking gold-colored spire.

909.

The Civic Center's design incorporates elements of organic architecture, blending harmoniously with the surrounding landscape.

910.

The Civic Center was added to the National Register of Historic Places in 1978.

911.

The construction of the Civic Center faced several challenges, including budget constraints and design modifications to accommodate seismic requirements.

912.

The Civic Center's roof design is reminiscent of sails or wings, reflecting the nearby natural beauty of the San Francisco Bay.

913.

The Civic Center's interior spaces feature innovative use of natural light, with large skylights and strategically placed windows.

914.

The Civic Center's design reflects Frank Lloyd Wright's philosophy of "organic architecture," which emphasizes harmony between the built environment and nature.

915.

The Civic Center's spacious grounds include landscaped gardens, reflecting pools, and outdoor seating areas.

916.

The Civic Center has been a popular filming location for movies and TV shows, including the iconic TV series "Star Trek."

917.

The Civic Center's Hall of Justice is home to the Marin County Superior Court and various county government offices.

918.

The Marin Center, located within the Civic Center complex, hosts a wide range of events, including concerts, trade shows, and community gatherings.

919.

The Civic Center has become an architectural landmark and a symbol of Marin County's civic pride.

920.

The Civic Center's design influenced the development of other buildings and structures around the world, inspiring architects and designers.

921.

The Civic Center's library features a vast collection of books, multimedia resources, and archival materials.

922.

The Civic Center's main auditorium, known as the Marin Veterans Memorial Auditorium, has a seating capacity of over 2,000 and hosts a variety of performances and events.

923.

The Civic Center's exterior was constructed using concrete and glass, giving it a modern and sleek appearance.

924.

The Civic Center's spacious lawn areas are often used for outdoor concerts, picnics, and community gatherings.

925.

The Civic Center's design takes into consideration energy efficiency and sustainable practices, including natural ventilation and solar orientation.

926.

The Civic Center's distinctive blue roof is made of glazed ceramic tiles, adding a vibrant touch to the overall design.

927.

The Civic Center's complex layout encourages pedestrian circulation, with interconnected walkways and open spaces.

928.

The Civic Center's rotunda features a beautiful circular staircase that leads to the upper levels of the building.

929.

The Civic Center's architecture reflects the mid-century modern style, characterized by clean lines, geometric shapes, and an integration with nature.

930.

The Civic Center's expansive windows provide panoramic views of the surrounding landscape and bring in ample natural light.

931.

The Civic Center has been a venue for public meetings, community forums, and civic engagement activities throughout its history.

932.

The Civic Center's design aimed to create a sense of unity and harmony among the various government departments and agencies housed within the complex.

933.

The Civic Center's construction was a collaborative effort involving architects, engineers, and contractors who worked closely with Frank Lloyd Wright to bring his vision to life.

934.

The Civic Center's design incorporates elements of Asian and Native American architectural influences, reflecting Frank Lloyd Wright's appreciation for different cultural traditions.

935.

The Civic Center's interior spaces are adorned with custom-designed furniture and fixtures, showcasing Frank Lloyd Wright's attention to detail.

936.

The Civic Center's library offers a variety of programs and services to the community, including storytime sessions, book clubs, and educational workshops.

937.

The Civic Center's landscaping features a diverse selection of native plants and trees, creating a tranquil and sustainable environment.

938.

The Civic Center's architectural design has been recognized and celebrated internationally, receiving accolades for its innovation and aesthetic appeal.

939.

The Civic Center's proximity to the Marinwood Plaza Shopping Center provides convenient access to amenities and services for visitors and employees.

940.

The Civic Center's grounds include walking paths and outdoor seating areas, encouraging people to enjoy the natural surroundings.

941.

The Civic Center's design incorporates elements of passive solar heating and cooling, maximizing energy efficiency and reducing environmental impact.

942.

The Civic Center's iconic rotunda serves as a symbol of Marin County's commitment to democracy, justice, and civic engagement.

943.

The Civic Center's open spaces and outdoor sculptures provide opportunities for artistic expression and cultural enrichment.

944.

The Civic Center's architectural design has been influential in shaping the development of public buildings and government complexes in subsequent years.

945.

The Civic Center's facilities are equipped with modern amenities and technology to support efficient government operations and public services.

946.

The Civic Center has been a venue for community celebrations, festivals, and cultural events that bring together residents and visitors.

947.

The Civic Center's design incorporates natural materials, such as wood and stone, creating a warm and inviting atmosphere.

948.

The Civic Center's sustainable design elements include rainwater harvesting systems and low-flow plumbing fixtures to minimize water consumption.

949.

The Civic Center's central plaza serves as a gathering place for community events, outdoor performances, and social gatherings.

950.

The Civic Center's architecture embodies Frank Lloyd Wright's vision of creating buildings that harmonize with their natural surroundings and inspire a sense of awe and appreciation.

951.

Mendocino Woodlands Recreational Demonstration Area is located in the heart of the Mendocino County, California, USA.

952.

It was established in 1934 as part of the New Deal program initiated by President Franklin D. Roosevelt.

953.

The area spans over 700 acres of lush redwood forest and is managed by the Mendocino Woodlands Camp Association.

954.

The Mendocino Woodlands was designed as a recreational space to provide affordable outdoor experiences for the public.

955.

It is listed on the National Register of Historic Places for its significant historical and cultural value.

956.

The Mendocino Woodlands showcases a unique architectural style known as "parkitecture," which blends seamlessly with the natural surroundings.

957.

The area features rustic cabins, lodges, and campsites that offer visitors a chance to disconnect from modern amenities and immerse themselves in nature.

958.

The Mendocino Woodlands was constructed using locally sourced materials, including redwood logs and stones.

959.

It served as a model for other recreational demonstration areas established during the Great Depression era.

960.

The Mendocino Woodlands offers a range of recreational activities, including hiking, nature walks, birdwatching, and camping.

961.

The area is home to diverse wildlife, including deer, foxes, raccoons, and a variety of bird species.

962.

The Mendocino Woodlands is a popular destination for educational and retreat programs, serving schools, universities, and community groups.

963.

During World War II, the area was used as a training ground for military personnel, emphasizing its versatility and adaptability.

964.

The Mendocino Woodlands has hosted numerous cultural and artistic events, such as music festivals, theater performances, and workshops.

965.

The area's amphitheater provides a scenic venue for outdoor concerts, plays, and other live performances.

966.

Several trails within the Mendocino Woodlands lead to scenic viewpoints, waterfalls, and serene picnic areas.

967.

The Mendocino Woodlands promotes environmental education and sustainability practices, offering programs that focus on ecology, conservation, and resource management.

968.

The area's natural beauty and tranquil atmosphere make it a popular choice for weddings, family gatherings, and special events.

969.

The Mendocino Woodlands has been an important site for historical research and documentation, providing insights into the development of recreational spaces in the United States.

970.

The area's proximity to the Pacific Ocean allows visitors to explore nearby coastal attractions, including beaches and tide pools.

971.

The Mendocino Woodlands has been recognized for its historical significance in preserving the legacy of the New Deal era and its impact on public recreation.

972.

The rustic cabins in the Mendocino Woodlands feature simple yet comfortable accommodations, allowing visitors to experience a back-to-nature lifestyle.

973.

The area's proximity to old-growth redwood forests provides visitors with the opportunity to witness the majestic beauty of these ancient trees.

974.

The Mendocino Woodlands has served as a backdrop for several films and documentaries, showcasing its scenic beauty and historical charm.

975.

The area's peaceful setting and lack of light pollution make it an excellent spot for stargazing and astronomy enthusiasts.

976.

The Mendocino Woodlands is managed by a dedicated team of volunteers and staff who work to preserve its natural and historical integrity.

977.

The area's rich cultural heritage is celebrated through interpretive exhibits, guided tours, and educational programs.

978.

The Mendocino Woodlands has been a source of inspiration for artists, writers, and musicians who seek creative inspiration in its serene and picturesque surroundings.

979.

The area's trails are well-maintained and offer varying levels of difficulty, catering to both casual walkers and experienced hikers.

980.

The Mendocino Woodlands has hosted outdoor education programs for children and youth, promoting environmental stewardship and fostering a love for nature.

981.

The area's historical significance lies not only in its architectural heritage but also in its role as a social experiment during the New Deal era.

982.

The Mendocino Woodlands provides a serene and secluded retreat from the hustle and bustle of city life, allowing visitors to recharge and reconnect with nature.

983.

The area's proximity to the Mendocino Headlands State Park and other natural attractions makes it an ideal base for exploring the region's natural wonders.

984.

The Mendocino Woodlands offers year-round recreational opportunities, with each season bringing its own unique charm and activities.

985.

The area's campsites are equipped with basic amenities, such as picnic tables, fire pits, and restroom facilities, ensuring a comfortable camping experience.

986.

The Mendocino Woodlands has been a site for historical reenactments, showcasing the lifestyle and activities of the early 20th-century campers.

987.

The area's peaceful ambiance and natural beauty have made it a favorite destination for meditation retreats and wellness programs.

988.

The Mendocino Woodlands has been recognized as a valuable resource for outdoor education, providing hands-on learning experiences for students of all ages.

989.

The area's old-growth redwoods are not only breathtaking to behold but also play a vital role in maintaining the region's ecosystem.

990.

The Mendocino Woodlands has inspired generations of nature enthusiasts, fostering a love and appreciation for the natural world.

991.

The area's historical significance extends beyond its recreational value, offering insights into the social and economic conditions of the Great Depression era.

992.

The Mendocino Woodlands has been a site for scientific research and ecological studies, contributing to our understanding of forest ecosystems and biodiversity.

993.

The area's diverse flora and fauna provide ample opportunities for nature photography and wildlife observation.

994.

The Mendocino Woodlands has been a place of refuge and solace for visitors seeking respite from the demands of modern life.

995.

The area's visitor center provides information on the history, ecology, and recreational opportunities available within the Mendocino Woodlands.

996.

The Mendocino Woodlands has been a catalyst for community engagement and volunteerism, encouraging people to take an active role in preserving and promoting the area's heritage.

997.

The area's natural trails offer an immersive experience, allowing visitors to connect with the sights, sounds, and scents of the redwood forest.

998.

The Mendocino Woodlands has been a site for cultural exchange, hosting international visitors who come to learn about American history and explore the natural beauty of the region.

999.

The area's proximity to Mendocino Village, known for its Victorian charm and coastal scenery, makes it an ideal stop for travelers exploring the region.

1000.

The Mendocino Woodlands continues to serve as a living testament to the ideals and aspirations of the New Deal era, providing a space for recreation, education, and appreciation of nature.